The King of the North at Jerusalem

God's People Delivered

The Relationship Between Daniel 11:45 and 12:1

Louis F. Were

The King of the North at Jerusalem

© 2002 by LMN Publishing International, Inc.

ISBN: 0-9665786-5-1

Published by:

Laymen Ministries

LMN Publishing International, Inc.
414 Zapada Rd.
St. Maries, ID 83861

Cover design by Terri Prouty

CONTENTS

Foreword 6

1. The Importance of the Right Understanding of Dan. 11:45; 12:1: "When the Books of Daniel and Revelation Are Better Understood".. 8

2. The Teaching of the Spirit of Prophecy and the Identity of the King of the North... 10

3. The Pioneers of the Advent Movement and the King of the North 12

4. Modern Babylon Comes to Its End; None Can Save It 16

5. Historical Reasons Why Turkey Could Not Be the King of the North 18

6. The Application of an Important Principle 23

7. The Principle of Parallel Passages: Comparing Scripture With Scripture 24

8. The Papacy—Not the French Revolution—Fulfills Dan. 11:36–40 ... 28

9. The Territory of the King of the North Defined by Scripture—Not by History Alone 36

10. The King of the North Is the King of Babylon 38

11. The King of the North Attacks God's Sanctuary 43

12. Other Principles of Interpretation Which Should Also Be Applied 47

13. Who Are Delivered at the Time the King of the North Comes to His End? Literal? Or Spiritual Israel?..................... 50

14. The New Covenant and the Interpretation of the Prophecy Concerning the King of the North 52

15. Interpreting Dan. 11:45 in Harmony With the New Covenant 56

16. "The Glorious Holy Mountain" 60

17. Jerusalem in the Prophecies: the Storm Centre of the Ages ... 62

18. North, South, East, and Egypt in Dan. 11:45 66

19. "These Shall Escape Out of His Hand, Even Edom, and Moab" (Dan. 11:41) 69

20. The New Testament Determines the Change From the Literal to the Spiritual in Old Testament Prophecies 71

21. The Enforcement of Sunday Laws Will Fulfill Daniel 11:45 ... 77

22. Will the Papacy Remove Its Seat of Power to the Literal City of Jerusalem? 82

23. Prophecy Points to Europe—Not Palestine—As the Storm Centre 85

24. When Will the King of the North Plant His Tabernacles at Jerusalem? 87

25. The King of the North Is Already Marshaling His Forces to Surround Jerusalem 91

26. Daniel's Last Prophecy Outlines the Great Controversy Between Christ and Satan 97

27. Why Daniel's Last Prophecy Was Given "By the Side of the Great River" (Dan. 10:4) 103

28. The King of the North Comes to His End: The Waters of the Euphrates Are Dried Up 106

29. Christ's Oath: The King of the North—Gog From the North Parts—Will Perish for Persecuting His People 110

30. The Time Periods of Daniel 12 Further Identify the Papacy As the King of the North... 115

"Thus saith the Lord, Stand ye in the ways, and see, and ask for *the old paths,* where is the good way, and walk therein" (Jer. 6:16).

"These are they which follow the Lamb whithersoever He goeth" (Rev. 14:4).

"All need wisdom carefully to search out the mystery of iniquity *that figures so largely* in the winding up of this earth's history"—*Testimonies to Ministers,* p. 118.

"There is nothing so powerful as truth—and often nothing so strange" —Daniel Webster.

KEY TO ABBREVIATIONS

1T, 2T, etc. . . . . *Testimonies,* Vol. 1, Vol. 2, etc.

AA . . . . *The Acts of the Apostles*

CT. . . . . *Counsels to Parents, Teachers, and Students*

DA . . . . *The Desire of Ages*

EW . . . . *Early Writings*

FE . . . . *Fundamentals of Christian Education*

GC . . . . *The Great Controversy*

PK . . . . *Prophets and Kings*

PP . . . . *Patriarchs and Prophets*

TM . . . . *Testimonies to Ministers*

**Note:* Page references to *Thoughts on Daniel and Revelation,* by Uriah Smith, may not coincide with more recent versions of that publication.

FOREWORD

"THEY THAT BE WISE"

A nd they that be wise [margin, 'teachers'] shall shine as the brightness of the firmament; and they that turn many to righteousness as the stars for ever and ever.

"But thou, O Daniel, shut up the words, and seal the book, even to the time of the end ['till the crisis at the end'—Moffatt]: many shall run to and fro, and knowledge shall be increased" (Dan. 12:3, 4).

The obvious connection between these two verses is that by teaching the things revealed in the book of Daniel, "they that be wise," or "teachers," will thus "turn many to righteousness," and have the joy in eternity of seeing the fruit of their labours. However, the book of Daniel, in the main, would not be thoroughly understood until toward "the crisis at the end." The nearer draws that "crisis," the more will the "wise," the "teachers" of "righteousness" (of which the unchangeable Law of God is the standard, Ps. 119:172; James 2:8–12, and about which the controversy revealed in Daniel's prophecies is being waged) "run to and fro" in their study of the book of Daniel; in this way their "knowledge" of Daniel and the Scriptures generally "shall be increased," and thus they will become more and more efficient in turning "many to righteousness." Enlightened and stimulated by their studies of Daniel and other Scriptures, their devotion to the cause of Christ will prompt them to travel to and fro throughout the earth spreading abroad the knowledge of His saving Grace and of all the truths of His Holy Word. The amazing inventions of modern times have been permitted by a wise Providence to enable the teachers of righteousness to quickly convey the Judgment-hour Message to all the world.

The method to be employed in the understanding of the book of Daniel is that of *"a turning to and fro in the prophecies, that is, a diligent and earnest search into prophetic truth"*—Uriah Smith's *Daniel and Revelation,* p. 312. See also *The Great Controversy,* pp. 356, 361, etc.

In the following pages, by adhering to this principle of *"turning to and fro in the prophecies,"* it has been possible to positively identify the power referred to in Dan. 11:40 as "the king of the north," and to interpret his activities, brought to view in verses 40–45, in relation to the deliverance of God's people mentioned in the very next verse (Dan. 12:1). By turning first to one prophecy of Daniel and then to another, and by comparing parallel passages—"comparing spiritual things with spiritual," as we are informed is the manner in "which the Holy Spirit teacheth" (1 Cor. 2:13; Isa. 28:9, 10; etc.)—and by comparing those passages again with others found in the Revelation and the Saviour's second advent sermon, it has been possible to make clear the great importance to the church of the inspired declaration that "the king of the north" would "come to his end" at Jerusalem. This prophecy is not one of secondary importance, but is vital to the people of God. The application of this prophecy presented in the Spirit of Prophecy is vindicated by the following analysis of Daniel's last prophecy.

—Louis F. Were.

Melbourne, Victoria, Australia.

5/11/49.

CHAPTER ONE

THE IMPORTANCE OF THE RIGHT UNDERSTANDING OF DAN. 11:45; 12:1

W*hen* the books of Daniel and Revelation are better understood. . ." (TM 114).

The identification of the king of the north is one of the most important themes that could possibly engage the attention of Seventh-day Adventists. As the end of the king of the north is the climax of Daniel's last prophecy, it is most important that we should be able to identify this power. When it is remembered that Daniel's last prophecy was given as the fitting conclusion to the very important prophecies which have preceded it, its importance will be seen. All the previous prophecies of Daniel have their consummation in this last prophecy. This prophecy was revealed to him after he had spent three weeks in fasting and praying in order to obtain clearer light on the previous prophecies. It is obvious, therefore, that unless we approach this subject in the light of the prophecies which have preceded it, we shall not understand aright the climax of them all—the ending of the king of the north at Jerusalem.

Concerning the interpretation of Daniel's previous prophecies Seventh-day Adventists are united. But the same unity is not maintained concerning the interpretation of Daniel's last prophecy—the reason for this is because the concluding portion of Daniel 11 (vs. 36–45) is not interpreted according to the same principle by which the previous parts are interpreted. When God's people apply this principle consistently, the unity manifested concerning the earlier prophecies of Daniel will also exist in regard to this last prophecy. When this time comes—as it surely will—there will be seen among us "a great *revival*," that "*great* revival" which the Lord's servant declares will come "*when* the books of Daniel and Revelation" are "*better* understood." TM 113, 114.

"*When* the books of Daniel and Revelation *are* better understood, believers will have *an entirely different religious experience.*"

TM 114. Surely this means more than a greater knowledge of the dates and historic features involved! Concerning the results to be accrued from a "better" understanding of the Apocalypse, we read: *"One thing* will certainly be understood from the study of the Revelation—that *the connection between God and His people is close and decided.* . . . The things revealed to Daniel were afterward complemented by the revelation made to John on the Isle of Patmos. These two books should be carefully studied." TM 114.

"To John were opened scenes of deep and thrilling interest in *the experience of the church.* He saw the position, dangers, conflicts, and *final deliverance* of the people of God. . . . Subjects of vast importance were revealed to him, *especially for the last church,* that those who should turn from error to truth might be instructed concerning the *perils and conflicts before them."* GC 341, 342.

From this inspired instruction we gather that there *will* come a time "when the books of Daniel and Revelation" will be *"better* understood," and *then* "will be seen among us a *great revival"* because a "better" understanding of these books will reveal the *nearness of God to His people.* We also learn that the Revelation is the complement of Daniel, so that a study of the Apocalypse will throw light on the book of Daniel. As shown later, this fact assists us in our understanding of Dan. 11:45.

In Daniel's previous prophecies the Lord had shown him the experiences through which the people of God would pass. In his three weeks' fasting and praying, Daniel sought the Lord for further revelations concerning the "dangers" and the "conflicts" of "the people of God." His prayer was answered in the light given him in his last prophecy. See Dan. 10:14. To interpret this prophecy in harmony with the express purpose for which it was given, requires a "better" understanding of "the books of Daniel and Revelation" than that which interprets the king of the north as Turkey. A right understanding of Dan. 11:40–45 concerning the ending of the king of the north at Jerusalem will be found to throw a flood of light upon other portions of the Scriptures that are vital to the Third Angel's Message: it will be found to contain a thrilling message of triumph for the people of God.

CHAPTER TWO

THE TEACHING OF THE SPIRIT OF PROPHECY
AND THE IDENTITY OF THE KING OF THE NORTH

Both Daniel and John foretold the "dangers, conflicts, and final *deliverance* [Dan. 12:1] of the people of God" (GC 341). John described these "dangers, conflicts, and final *deliverance* of the people of God" in connection with the Satanic forces of spiritual Babylon (Rev. 13 to 19). Daniel described the same things in connection with the "king of the north."

Our attention should be arrested by the fact that, in the scores of places where the Lord's servant refers to Daniel's prophecy of the *deliverance* of God's people, greatly enlarging upon the theme in her graphic descriptions of that great event, she does not make the slightest reference to the ending of Turkey! For instance, read chapters 40 and 41 of *The Great Controversy* concerning "God's People Delivered," and observe that this deliverance of the people of God is described in connection with the judgments which fall upon Babylon. In *Early Writings*, pp. 282–285, in the chapter, "The Time of Trouble," God's servant invariably speaks of the *deliverance* of God's people in connection with the enforcement of Babylon's false Sabbath and the attempt to slay the Lord's people for their loyalty to the Law of God. Not the slightest reference is made to Turkey's doom! Yet in Dan. 11:45; 12:1 the ending of the king of the north is mentioned in connection with the deliverance of God's people! The obvious conclusion derived from this association is that the king of the north is responsible for the "dangers" and "conflicts" of the church, and that it is his evil work against the church which necessitates the Lord's intervention to bring "*deliverance*" to His people.

As the king of the north does the same work as the Papacy there can be but one conclusion, namely, that the king of the north refers to the Papacy. Thus we see why John the Revelator and the servant of the Lord describe "the final deliverance of the people of

God" *while describing God's judgments upon spiritual Babylon.* Daniel, John, and the Spirit of Prophecy are in perfect agreement!

When this truth is seen by God's people "there will be seen among us a great revival," for it requires "a better knowledge of the books of Daniel and Revelation" to understand thoroughly *why* the king of the north is the Papacy and to know *how* he comes to his end at Jerusalem. To understand the prophecies given to him, Daniel fasted and prayed for three weeks (Dan. 10:2, 3). John "wept much" (Rev. 5:4) because of his intense longing for a true understanding of the revelations given to him. When God's people engage in fasting and praying and weeping, with intense longing to have "a better knowledge of the books of Daniel and the Revelation," they will see that the king of the north *could not possibly be* Turkey but that, undoubtedly, it is the Papacy that comes to "his end" *because of its persecution of the people of God.*

CHAPTER THREE

THE PIONEERS OF THE ADVENT MOVEMENT AND THE KING OF THE NORTH

The godly pioneers of the Advent Movement, from their consecrated study of the Word of God, came to the conclusion that the power referred to in the closing verses of Dan. 11 was the Papacy. Their belief they expressed in *A Word to the Little Flock*, p. 9. After quoting Dan. 12:1 we read: "This last power that treads the saints is brought to view in Revelation 13:11–18. His number is 666."

In the *Signs of the Times* (edited by James White) of July 22, 1880, Elder James White wrote: "The field of Daniel's prophecy embraces five universal kingdoms. These are Babylon, Medo-Persia, Grecia, and Rome, and the eternal kingdom of God. The ground of the four perishable kingdoms, reaching to, and introducing the immortal kingdom, is covered by four distinct lines of prophecy. These are given in chapters two, seven, eight, and eleven. The eleventh chapter of Daniel closes with the close of the fourth monarchy with these words: [Dan. 11:45 and 12:1–3 are then quoted].

"The student of prophecy is thus borne down the stream of time from Babylon in the height of the glory of that kingdom, past Media and Persia, the kingdom of Grecia, and *the Roman Empire which comes to its end at the second coming of Christ.*"

Condemning the view that Turkey was the power referred to in Dan. 11:40–45, James White wrote an editorial in the *Review and Herald,* November 29, 1877. He said: "Let us take a brief view of the *line of prophecy four times spanned* in the book of Daniel. It will be admitted that the same ground is passed over in chapters two, seven, eight, and eleven, with this exception, that Babylon is left out of chapters eight and eleven. We first pass down the great image of chapter 2, where Babylon, Persia, Greece, and Rome are represented by the gold, the silver, the brass, and the iron. All agree that *these feet are not Turkish but Roman.* And as we pass down to the lion, the bear, the leopard, and the beast with ten horns, representing the same as the great image, again all will agree that it is *not Turkey that is cast into the burning flame, but the Roman beast.* So of chapter 8, all agree that the little horn that stood up against the Prince of princes is *not Turkey but Rome.* In *all* these lines thus far *Rome is the last form of government mentioned."* (Emphasis mine.)

"*Now comes the point in the argument upon which very much depends. Does the eleventh chapter of the prophecy of Daniel cover the ground measured by chapters two, seven, and eight? If so, then the last power mentioned in that chapter is Rome."* (Emphasis his.)

In a sermon on Daniel 11 delivered by Uriah Smith at Battle Creek, Michigan, he introduced the new interpretation bringing Turkey into the prophecy. At that time James White said: "Elder Smith has given a very fine talk on the eleventh chapter of Daniel, and his interpretation seems plausible, but IF the legs of iron, and the feet of iron and clay in the second chapter represent Rome, and IF the nondescript, ten-horned beast, and the little horn of the seventh chapter represent Rome, and IF the little horn which waxed exceeding great of the eighth chapter represents Rome, the King of the North represents Rome also. These are four parallel prophecies, brethren, reaching down to the coming of our Lord." (Quoted in *King of the North,* by M. C. Wilcox, Mountain View, California, 1910, page 44.)

In his paper, "The Pioneers on Daniel Eleven and Armaged-don" (presented to the Bible Research Fellowship), Raymond F. Cottrell says: "From 1844 to 1875. . . the pioneers of the message were united in their understanding of the king of the north and Armageddon." After presenting documentary evidence, Cottrell further says: "In summary, the battle of Armageddon as under-stood by the pioneers consisted in the people of God being attacked by the wicked but delivered by Christ and His angels. There is no hint of Armageddon being a conflict of nation against nation." Referring to an editorial by James White in the *Review and Herald,* Vol. XIX. No. 8, January 21, 1862, p. 61, entitled "Thoughts on the Great Battle," Cottrell again summarizes: "The denominational view had not changed since the publication of the hymn ten years earlier. Armageddon was still a battle 'between earth and heaven' rather than one 'between nation and nation.' A little later in the same year an editorial by Elder Smith appeared in the *Review and Herald,* Vol. XIX, No. 24, May 18, 1862, p. 192, commenting briefly on Dan. 11:45, in which it is evident that he understood that prophecy in harmony with the contemporary denominational view of Armageddon. First, he quotes a current news item [regarding the]. . . 'plan of *removing the seat of the Papacy to Jerusalem.'*

"Immediately following the quotation appears the laconic comment, 'Is not the above item significant, taken in connection with Dan. 11:45?' That is all! He simply takes it for granted that everyone will agree with him in recognizing Rome as the power indicated in the last verse of Daniel 11. The brief, direct, matter-of-fact tone of his comment is the best possible evidence that the leaders of that time held unanimously to the original denominational position. . . .

"By 1877 Uriah Smith had shifted from his original position and substituted Turkey for Rome. James White ['in an editorial in the pages of the *Review* dated November 29, 1877'] advised caution in the interpretation of unfulfilled prophecy and found Uriah Smith 'removing the landmarks fully established in the Advent Movement.' The article makes it clear that the position making Rome the power of Daniel 11:45 and Rev. 16:12 had been 'fully established' as a 'landmark' in the Advent Movement up to that time."

In the following pages, the writer demonstrates the accuracy of the interpretation, unanimously held by the Seventh-day Adventist denomination for "the first third of the century since 1844," that the Papacy is referred to in Dan. 11:45. The position presented by James White is positively Scriptural, and his protests against the introduction of the new ideas on Armageddon relating to Turkey and a supposed military war to fulfill the prophecies of Dan. 11:45; Rev. 16:12; etc., are abundantly justified. The line of reasoning presented by James White in justification of the belief of Seventh-day Adventists, held by them for so long a time, is faultless, and is supported by all the laws of interpretation revealed within the Scriptures themselves.

As is well known to Bible students, the number four is employed throughout the Scriptures where it is designed to emphasize the world-wide scope of the prophecy. In the book of Daniel there are *four* worldly "universal" kingdoms brought to view: Babylon, Medo-Persia, Grecia and Rome. These four kingdoms are represented as "*four* great beasts" rising as "the *four* winds of the heaven strove upon the great sea." *Four* world rulers are specifically named: Nebuchadnezzar, Belshazzar, Darius and Cyrus. *Four* great lines of prophecy stretch from the days of the prophet to the end of worldly kingdoms: Dan. 2, 7, 8, 11. If Papal Rome were not mentioned in the closing verses of Daniel 11, that prophecy would not for the fourth time cover the same course of history already mentioned three times. In the record of the sermon the Saviour delivered respecting the destruction of Jerusalem and pointing to the end of the world (a sermon based upon the book of Daniel, see Matt. 24:15, etc.), we are explicitly informed of the

names of only *four* of His disciples who were then present: "Peter
and James and John and Andrew" (Mark 13:3).

Each of Daniel's four lines of prophecy *ends with world-wide
events:* In chapter two, the Stone, representing the establishment of
the Saviour's kingdom, at His second advent, destroys all the
kingdoms of the world; in chapter 7, the Saviour destroys the
world-wide power of spiritual Rome; in chapters 8 and 9 the same
fact is repeated, and in chapter 12:1, 2, it will not be denied, world-
wide events are outlined to occur at the time when the king of the
north comes to his end. "At that time shall Michael stand up,"
"there shall be a time of trouble," "at that time Thy people shall be
delivered"—these are to be worldwide in scope. Surely logic
demands that as each of Daniel's outlines ends with world-wide
events, so the ending of the king of the north, as well as the other
events mentioned to occur when he comes to his end, should also
refer to something worldwide.

Interpreting Dan. 11:45 to mean the ending of Turkey magnifies
a comparatively small national event to disproportionate significance,
and also introduces something not only totally incongruous to all that
is revealed in the terminals of the other prophecies, but also something totally incongruous to the other world events to transpire at the
time when the king of the north comes to his end.

The last prophecy, particularly, was given to declare what
would "befall" God's people "in the latter days" (Dan. 10:14), and
surely no revelation concerning the experiences of the church
would be complete without also revealing the work and defeat of
their enemies. Thus the king of the north must refer to that power
whose persecution necessitates the *"deliverance"* of God's people,
and for which persecutions he will suffer the wrath of the Lord of
the church. Would it not indicate a lack of wisdom for God to give
a prophecy, declaring that its purpose is to show what would
"befall" the church "in the latter days" and, *pointing to her deliverance,* spend so much space in His Word—especially at the climax of
the spiritual conflict—describing the downfall of a small nation
totally disconnected with that "deliverance?"

There is nothing in the Word of God to support the belief that
Turkey is the power referred to in Dan. 11:45, but all Scripture
unitedly and most emphatically declares that that power who
comes to his end, as declared in verse 45, is the Papacy—spiritual
Babylon. The Pioneers were right! The Seventh-day Adventist
denominational view held unanimously for a third of a century is
the correct Scriptural view. It is surely time that there was a return
to the "landmark fully established in the Advent Movement."

CHAPTER FOUR

MODERN BABYLON COMES TO ITS END; NONE CAN SAVE IT

That the phrase "he shall come to his end, and none shall help him" has reference to the overthrow of modern Babylon is evident when compared with other passages of Scripture which definitely refer to the doom of Babylon. Concerning the doom of Babylon, the prophet Isaiah wrote: "Mischief shall fall upon thee; *thou shalt not be able to put it off*. . . . Let now the astrologers, the stargazers, the monthly prognosticators, stand up, and *save thee from these things* that shall come upon thee. . . . *None shall save thee*." Isa. 47:1, 11–15. In Isa. 47 the doom of Babylon is portrayed in unmistakable language, and this is one of the chapters from which John, in the book of Revelation, quotes in his description of the overthrow of spiritual Babylon. See verses 7, 8, 9, 11, 14, 15 of Isa. 47, and note the marginal references to Rev. 18. Paul, also, quotes from this chapter (Isa. 47) when referring to the destruction of modern Babylon. Three statements in 1 Thess. 5:3 definitely connect with the overthrow of ancient Babylon:

(1) "Sudden destruction" (Isa. 47:9, 11; Jer. 51:8; 50:44).

(2) "As travail upon a woman with child" (Jer. 50:43, 44; see also Isa. 13:1, 6–8).

(3) "And th*ey shall not escape*"—"Thou shalt not be able to put it off. . . *none shall save thee*" (Isa. 47:11–15).

Thus Daniel's statement that modern Babylon "shall come to his end, but none shall help him" harmonizes with the inspired statements of other Bible writers who declare the doom of Babylon in similar language.

Throughout the book of Daniel the overthrow of Babylon is described: In chapter two the stone descends upon the ten toes which stand upon Europe, where Babylon is centred. (See also Rev. 17:12–14.) The doom of spiritual Babylon is prefigured in the overthrow of literal Babylon by Cyrus, the night of Belshazzar's blasphemous feast. The close of probation for that nation is a type of the close of probation for spiritual Babylon, for when modern Babylon makes a blasphemous use of the things of God's temple—enforcing the Papal Sabbath in lieu of the Sabbath of God's Commandment—their probation will end and no one will be able to help them. The Divine judgments upon modern Babylon, for its evil work against the Sabbath and for persecuting the saints, is mentioned in Daniel 7, and again in chapter 8:25, where we read: "But he shall be broken without hand." See also Dan. 9:27. Thus the judgment of God which falls upon the king of the north refers, not to some military defeat, but to the almighty power of God, against which no help from man could possibly preserve the persecutors of His people.

A comparison of Dan. 8:25 and Dan. 11:45 reveals that both refer to the Papacy. Daniel 8:25 declares: "He shall also *stand up against the Prince* of princes; *but* he shall be broken without hand." "Yet under one head—the Papal power—the people will unite to *oppose God in the person of His witnesses*." 7T 182. This is what is taught in Dan. 11:44, 45: "He shall stand up against the Prince of princes"—"in the person of His witnesses"—"*yet* he shall come to his end, and none shall help him," "he shall be broken without hand."

CHAPTER FIVE

HISTORICAL REASONS WHY TURKEY COULD NOT BE THE KING OF THE NORTH

The Ottoman Empire, in the past, could not have been the king of the north: the Turkish Republic, in the present, could not be the king of the north. The facts of Turkish history will not fit the prophetic mould. Those who still believe that this power is the king of the north, evidently appalled by all that is implied by the belief that Turkey will yet move its seat of government to Jerusalem, say little or nothing concerning this feature of their interpretation of Dan. 11:45. *Yet this is the climax of the prophecy.* Because this power pitches "the tabernacles of his palace" "in the glorious holy mountain," the exclamation is brought forth *"yet* he shall come to his end, and none shall help him." Though the power mentioned in the prophecy is so mighty that it actually pitches its tabernacles at Jerusalem—the very heart of strength and power— yet, despite his great power thus demonstrated, "he shall come to his end"—as will be shown later, by the irresistible power of God.

Is there anything in the world today to indicate that Turkey would be strong enough to fuse together the great territories which formerly belonged to the king of the north? Is there anything in the world today to suggest, even remotely, that America, Great Britain, the United Nations Organization, or any other power or nation, desires to see Turkey in possession of Jerusalem? Would the Papacy that reaps a harvest of cash from its "holy" (?) places desire to see Turkey established there? Have they forgotten the "Crusades?" Would America, whose foreign policy, today, is so influenced by Vatican pressure, permit little Turkey to regain possession of Jerusalem? Does Turkey have any plan or thought of going to Jerusalem? The teaching that Turkey is the king of the north win not meet the specifications of the prophecy.

The prophecy of Dan. 11:43 says of the king of the north: "The Libyans and the Ethiopians shall be at his steps." In Ex. 11:8, margin, the same expression is employed when referring to the Israelites acting under the government of Moses. See also

Judg. 4:10; 1 Kings 20:10, margin; 2 Kings 3:9, margin, etc. The Ethiopians were never under the government of Turkey; they were never at the steps of Turkey. Gibbon says, that after the seventh century, "Compassed by the enemies of their religion, the Ethiopians slept for near a thousand years, forgetful of the world by whom they were forgotten."

The prophecy also declares (Dan. 11:40): "At the time of the end shall the king of the south *push* at him." In support of the belief that Turkey is the king of the north, it is said that in 1798 "Egypt did 'push,' or make a comparatively feeble resistance" against France. When we permit the Bible to be its own expositor, we learn from the use Daniel has already made of the word "push" that it is employed to describe a power that is vigorous and successful in its campaign. In Dan. 7:4 we read: "I saw the ram *pushing* westward, and northward, and southward; so that *no beasts might stand before him,* neither was there any that could deliver out of his hand." Egypt's feeble resistance of the French in 1798 did not fulfill the prophecy of Dan. 11:40 and the king of the north that was prophesied to "come against him like a whirlwind" could not be that of Turkey's resistance to the French invasion of her territory.

The belief that in 1798 Turkey was "the king of the north" and Egypt "the king of the south" seems very incongruous, because Egypt was then included in Turkish territory. Writing of Napoleon's invasion of Egypt in 1798, H. G. Wells says: "Moreover, *Egypt was a part of the Turkish Empire."—Outline of History,* Vol. II, page 584. Why should Turkey and territory governed by her vassal be regarded as two separate powers?

Another incongruity appears when applying the term "the king of the north" or "the king of the south" to the powers conquering the respective territories. By this principle, when France occupied Egypt it should have become "the king of the south"— thus there would not be three powers to engage in the so-called "triangular" war of 1798, in supposed fulfillment of Dan. 11:40!

The belief that Turkey is the king of the north is based upon the teaching that Dan. 11:40 outlines "a triangular war." A close analysis of that verse shows that there are only two powers brought to view, namely, the king of the north and the king of the south. The pronoun "him" referring firstly to the king of the north whose activities have been described in the previous verses. The king of the south who pushes at "him" is referred to in the second "him," for it is against "him," the king of the south, that the king of the north comes. The *Septuagint Version* reads: "And at the time of the end the king of Egypt shall push at him, and the king of the north shall be enraged at him, with chariots and many horses and many ships, and shall enter into the land of Egypt." The *American Translation* reads: "At the time of the end the king of the south shall thrust at him; but the king of the north shall burst upon him like a whirlwind, with many chariots, and horsemen, and many ships, and shall sweep through many lands like an overwhelming flood."

The teaching that Dan. 11:40 describes "a triangular war" is created by interfering with the actual wording of the Scripture. Verse 36 reads: "And *the* king shall do according to his will; and he shall exalt himself, and magnify himself above every god, and shall speak marvelous things against the God of gods." These are the verses quoted by Paul in 2 Thess. 2:3, 4, when describing the Papacy. It is freely admitted that the Papacy is clearly outlined in verses 31–35 of Dan. 11, and the natural reading of the Scripture would be in harmony with the application made by Paul of v. 36, namely, that the Papacy is thus described. To bring in another power—France—to make up the three in a supposed "triangular war" (though the text [v. 40] only speaks of two), it has been necessary to change the definite article "*the* king" to "*a* king." But it is perfectly obvious that this forcing of the Scripture to say something different from what it does say, has been necessary to find support for the wrong application of v. 40. Thus, as it always happens in the interpretation of Scriptures, one mistake leads to another.

Regarding the "triangular war:" after having misapplied verses 36–39 to refer to France instead of to the Papacy, could it strictly be said to be "a triangular war" when England was also at war with France and assisted the Turks against the French? As stated in *Daniel and Revelation*, p. 282: "Sir Sidney Smith at the same time appeared before St. Jean d'Acre with two English ships, *reinforced the Turkish garrison* of that place, and *captured the apparatus for the siege,* which Napoleon had sent round by sea from Alexandria. A Turkish fleet soon appeared in the offing, which, *with the Russian and English vessels then co-operating with them,* constituted the 'many ships' of the king of the north." (Emphasis mine.) It is not strictly true that it was "a triangular war." The truth of God's Word does not require weak if not contradictory evidence for its support.

The prophecy of Dan. 11:40–45, in a most arresting manner, depicts the successful conquests of an almost irresistible conqueror. After recovering from an attack by the king of the south, the king of the north embarks upon a campaign that meets with almost overwhelming success. He would attack "like a whirlwind," everything would be subordinated to his lust for power— "chariots," "horsemen" and "many ships" would be under his control to sweep him forward to success. Like the overflowing of a mighty river, he would "enter into the countries, and shall overflow and pass over. He shall enter also into the glorious land [compare Dan. 8:9; 11:16], and many countries shall be overthrown." The prophecy proceeds to outline the vastness of his conquests. Coming from the north, he would continue his victorious march of conquests until he reached and conquered nations which, in those days of slow locomotion, were far-removed to the south—Egypt, Libya and Ethiopia.

These mighty conquests were to be subsequent to an attack made upon him "at the time of the end." Instead of the history of Turkey fitting these prophetic specifications, her history is the very reverse. Turkey had been in Palestine for centuries and her conquests were prior to "the time of the end."

The Turkish Empire attained the highest pinnacle of its glory during the 16th century. Then, it was young and vigorous, and at the height of its power. But the great empire, which had been built up by warrior Sultans, soon began to decay under the rulership of their sensuous successors. Early in the 17th century the empire seemed almost at the point of dissolution. Towards the close of the seventeenth century European powers, including the Pope, allied themselves in a general coalition against the Turkish Empire. Having been weakened by constant war with these European powers and Russia, the Ottomans were unable to muster sufficient strength, and acting upon the advice of England, the Turkish Sultan agreed to sign the peace of Karlowitz in January, 1699. Since that treaty was signed the Turkish Empire has suffered continuously from decay, and has been subjected to the most humiliating and ignominious treatment at the hands of European powers.

The prophecy (Dan. 11:40–45) calls for feats of warlike strength which Turkey did not accomplish at any time (at least, as concerning Ethiopia), and which could never have been accomplished in the nineteenth century when the Turk was universally regarded as "the sick man of the East;" and when his tottering empire was only held together because the European powers were too jealous of each other to permit anyone of them to destroy the decaying empire of the Sultan. When "the time of the end" commenced, Turkey was decaying rapidly. Instead of meeting the specifications of the prophecy by being robust, strong and vigorous, adding conquests to conquests until able to "go forth with great fury to destroy, and utterly to make away many" Turkey, since the commencement of "the time of the end," has continued to be "the sick man of the East."

When interpreted militarily, the prophecy declares that the king of the north, subsequent to an attack from the king of the south, would "enter also into the glorious land." But Turkey had conquered Palestine in the 16th century and was still in possession of it in 1798. This further illustrates the utter misapplication of the prophecy to Turkey. Instead of Turkey establishing her government at Jerusalem she lost the whole of Palestine in the first World War. It was formerly quite generally believed that some day, probably as a result of Russian aggression, the Turk would be driven out of Europe, from whence he would flee *to* Jerusalem. But the flight of Turkey in 1917 was not South *to* Jerusalem, but North *from* it!

Dan 11:41 declares that "Edom shall escape out of his hand." In fulfillment of prophecy (such as Obadiah 18, etc.), the Edomites as a separate people have not existed for over a thousand years— how, then, could a non-existent people escape out of the hands of Turkey? How the Edomites escape out of the hands of the Papacy will be shown later.

These historical facts show that the prophecy cannot be interpreted aright in relation to Turkey. These and other incongruities do not appear when the prophecy is interpreted in harmony with New Testament teaching.

CHAPTER SIX

THE APPLICATION OF AN IMPORTANT PRINCIPLE

T he track of time is strewn with the wreckage of false interpretations of prophecy. At one time, because they appeared superficially based upon some Scripture, many of them were widely accepted. From them, Bible expositors should learn the important lesson: "Knowing this first, that no prophecy of the Scripture is of any *private* interpretation" (2 Pet. 1:20). This means that the Scriptures must expound themselves. No teaching is to be accepted that is a human deduction from a passage of Scripture. No interpretation is to be derived from isolating the passage concerned from all that the Word of God has given elsewhere. The Westminster Confession declares: "The infallible rule of interpretation of Scripture is the Scripture itself. . . It must be searched and known from other places that speak more clearly."

The Lord's counsel to His people is: "Investigate, *compare Scripture with Scripture,* sink the shaft of truth down deep into the mine of God's Word." We must *"make the Bible its own expositor."* TM 476, 106. "Precept must be upon precept; line upon line; here a little, and there a little" (Isa. 28:9, 10). "Words. . . which the Holy Ghost teacheth; *comparing spiritual things with spiritual"* (1 Cor. 2:13). Only in this way can man be sure that his teachings are from the Lord, and that he thus has "the testimony of Jesus."

When this simple but effective test is applied to the belief that Turkey is the king of the north, it fails completely, for there are no other passages in the book of Daniel which make even the slightest reference to Turkey; there are no other passages in any other part of the Bible applying the words in Daniel's last prophecy to Turkey. Thus standing alone, that interpretation is shown to be a *"private* interpretation." However, by comparing Scripture with Scripture we see that Paul, when describing the Papacy in 2 Thess. 2:3, 4, quotes from Dan. 11:36–38, so that the power referred to must be the Papacy. Again, when applying this test within the book of Daniel itself, the belief that the Papacy is the power referred to is supported by the fact that the Papacy looms large in Daniel's previous prophecies, and also that they, too, end with the destruction of Rome as the enemy of God and His people. As shown elsewhere, the destruction of the king of the north is described in similar terms to that describing the destruction of spiritual Babylon.

CHAPTER SEVEN

THE PRINCIPLE OF PARALLEL PASSAGES: COMPARING SCRIPTURE WITH SCRIPTURE

A COMPARISON OF THE ENDINGS OF DANIEL'S PROPHECIES SHOWING THAT THEY ALL END WITH THE DOOM OF BABYLON.

Dan. 2:33, 34, 43–45. The stone ("cut out of the mountains without hands"), representing the second coming of Christ, falls upon the ten toes of the Babylonian image. Those ten toes represent the nations of Europe under the leadership of the Papacy. See Dan. 7:7, 8, 20, 24; Rev. 17:12–14.

Dan. 7:11, 26. The Roman beast is destroyed at the second advent. "The beast was slain." "To consume and to destroy it unto the end."

Dan. 8:25. The Roman desolator "shall be broken without hand"— that is, without any human help—none shall help him.

Dan. 9:27, margin. "That determined shall be poured upon the desolator."

Dan. 11:45. "Yet he shall come to his end, and none shall help him."

How utterly incongruous it would be for Daniel to give a series of prophecies ending in the destruction of the forces of Babylon that have opposed the work and people of God, to end up his last, *the climax of them all,* describing the end of a comparatively small nation having no direct relationship with the great conflict which he has portrayed in progress down through the centuries until the second advent! But how fitting for him to climax all that he has written by giving a vivid presentation of the final phases of the spiritual conflict, which ends in the utter destruction of the enemies of God and of His people. Such a presentation harmonizes with what other Bible writers have written—see 2 Thess. 2:3, 8; Rev. 16:12–16; 17:14; chapter 18; 19:11–21.

A COMPARISON OF DANIEL'S LAST TWO PROPHECIES SHOWING THAT HIS LAST PROPHECY IS AN EXPLANATION OF THE FORMER

The following parallels will show at a glance that Daniel's last prophecy (10 to 12) was given as an enlargement and explanation of his previous prophecy (8 and 9). In both these prophecies the same historical features are considered: Medo-Persia; Grecia and its break up; Rome's invasion of "the pleasant," or "glorious land;" Papal Rome's war against the Lord's sanctuary and His people, and both end with the doom of the Papacy. Dan. 9:1 and Dan. 11:1 both refer to "the first year of Darius," in 538 B.C. Darius, however, was dead when Daniel had this dream; Cyrus then being the sole monarch of the kingdom (Dan. 10:1).

THE VISION OF DANIEL 8		THE VISION OF DANIEL 10–12	
v. 3, 20	"KINGS OF MEDIA AND PERSIA"	11: 2	"KINGS IN PERSIA"
v. 5, 21	"GRECIA"	v. 2, 3	"GRECIA"
v. 8	"Strong"	v. 3	"A mighty king"
v. 8	"waxed very great"	v. 3	"rule with great dominion"
v. 8	"great horn was broken"	v. 4	"kingdom shall be broken"
v. 8	"toward the four winds of heaven"	v. 4	"toward the four winds of heaven"
		v. 5–13	Additional features given concerning the break up of Grecia: Conflicts of the kings of north and south
v. 9	ROME: A little horn arises "out of one of them"—the territory of the king of the north	v. 16	ROME:
		v. 15	came against "the king of the north." Syria conquered and added to the Roman Empire, B.C. 65
v. 9	"waxed exceeding great"	v. 16	"None shall stand before him"
v. 9	"toward the pleasant or glorious land"	v. 16	"shall stand in the glorious land"
v. 10	"Stamped upon" the Jews	v. 14	"The robbers or breakers of thy people" (see also Dan. 12:7, R.V.)
v. 11	"against the Prince of the host" (margin)	v. 22	"The Prince of the Covenant" to be "broken"
		v. 16–30	Additional features given concerning pagan Rome
v. 11	"By him the daily was taken away"	v. 31	"Shall take away the daily"
v. 11	God's "sanctuary was cast down"	v. 31	"shall pollute the sanctuary"
v. 12	"cast down the truth"	v. 31–35	Persecuted those who stood for truth
v. 12	"practised and prospered"	v. 36	"shall prosper"
v. 13	"the transgression of desolation"	v. 31	"the abomination that maketh desolate"

v. 13	"both the sanctuary and the host to be trodden under foot"	v. 31–35; Rev. 11:2	"The holy city ["the true church" GC 266] shall they tread under foot forty and two months"
v. 13	"How long?"	12:6	"How long?"
v. 14	"Unto 2,300 days"	12:7, 11, 12	"At the end of the days"—1260, 1290, 1335. Details given when Papal supremacy would begin and end
v. 17	"The time of the end"	11:35, 40; 12:4, 9	"The time of the end"
v. 19	"the last end of the indignation"	11:36	"till the indignation be accomplished"
v. 19	"at the time appointed the end shall be"	11:27, 35	"the end shall be at the time appointed"
v. 23	"when the trangressors are come to the full"	12:10	"the wicked shall do wickedly"
v. 24	"his power shall be mighty"	11:31–35	Destroyed God's people in Dark Ages; when power restored in last days he will amass forces to slay the saints (vs. 40–45)
v. 24	"he shall destroy wonderfully;" "destroy the mighty and the holy people"	11:31–35	killed millions of God's people in Dark Ages; see also v. 44
v. 25	"shall cause to prosper"	11:32	"shall corrupt by flatteries"
v. 25	"he shall magnify himself"	11:36	"the king [of the north] shall...magnify himself"
v. 25	"he shall stand up against the Prince of princes"	11:36	"against the God of gods"
v. 25	"but he shall be broken without hand"	11:45	"yet he shall come to his end, and none shall help him"
v. 25,	"THE VISION"	10:1	THE VISION: "a thing was revealed"
v. 26	"is true"	10:1	"the thing was true"
v. 26	"shut thou up the vision"	12:4, 9	"shut up the words"
v. 26	"it shall be for many days"	10:14	"for yet the vision is for many days"
v. 27	THE UNDERSTANDING OF THE VISION	10:1	THE UNDERSTANDING OF THE VISION
v. 27	"none understood it"	10:1	Daniel "understood the thing, and had understanding of the vision"

Daniel's introduction to his last prophecy (10:1) shows that, with this prophecy, the things he did not understand regarding the previous vision were made clear to him: he then "understood the thing, and had understanding of the vision." Had the Lord mentioned other matters not included in his previous vision (details concerning the French Revolution and Turkey) He would have added more problems for Daniel to solve. However, in Daniel's last vision *only* that is mentioned which enlarges upon the powers brought to view in his previous prophecies.

Notice particularly how both these prophecies end:

Dan. 8:25 "He shall also stand up against the Prince of princes BUT

Dan. 8:25 "He shall be broken without hand" "Without hand" means without human aid, see Dan. 2:45; 2 Cor. 5:1; etc. Therefore "none shall help him."

Dan. 11:45 "He shall plant the tabernacle of his palace" outside Jerusalem YET

Dan. 11:45 "He shall come to his end, and none shall help him."

CHAPTER EIGHT

THE PAPACY—NOT THE FRENCH REVOLUTION—FULFILLS DAN. 11:36–40

Expressions employed concerning the king of the north, when compared with other Scriptures which are known to refer to the Papacy, show he is the Papacy:

IN DANIEL'S LAST PROPHECY—		OTHER SCRIPTURES—
11:36	"The king [of the north]"	The Papacy
11:36	"exalt himself"	2 Thess. 2:4 "Exalteth himself." See also Isa. 14:13; Dan. 11:14; GC 50.
11:36	"The king...shall magnify himself above every god."	Dan. 8:25 "He shall magnify himself in his heart"
		Dan. 8:11 "He magnified himself even to the Prince of the host."
11:36	"Shall speak marvelous things against the God of gods"	Dan. 7:25 "Shall speak great words against the Most High"
		Rev. 13:5 "And there was given unto him a mouth speaking great things and blasphemies." See also Dan. 7:8, 11, 20.
11:36	"Shall prosper"	Dan. 8:12 "It practised and prospered"
		Dan. 8:24 "And shall prosper and practise"
		Dan. 7:25 "Shall think to change times and laws"
11:36	"Shall prosper till the indignation be accomplished"	Rev. 14:9, 10 "If any man worship the beast...the wrath of God...His indignation." See also Isa. 13:5; Jer. 50:25.
Amer. Trans.—"He shall prosper till the time of wrath is ended"		Dan. 7:11 "I beheld even till the beast was slain, and his body destroyed"
		GC 579 "Paul states plainly that the man of sin will continue until the second advent."
11:37	"Neither shall he regard the God of his fathers"	2 Thess. 2:4 "Who opposeth and exalteth himself above all that is called God." See Rev. 17:13, 14.

11:37 "Nor the desire of women"

1 Tim. 4:1–3 "Shall depart from the faith...forbidding to marry"

11:37 "Nor regard any god: for he shall magnify himself above *all*"

2 Thess. 2:4 "Who opposeth and exalteth himself above *all* that is called God, or that is worshipped."

The translators were correct in placing this verse in the margin of Dan. 11:37. By thinking to change God's Law, the Papacy has not regarded God's desires.

11:38 "But in his estate shall he honour the God of forces"

Dan. 8:24 "And his power shall be mighty, but not by is own power; and he shall destroy wonderfully"

Dan. 11:31 "And arms shall stand on his part"

Rev. 18:24 "And in her was found the blood of prophets, and of the saints, and of all that were slain upon the earth."

Lord Acton, R. C. historian, says: "The Papacy contrived murder and massacre on the largest and also on the most cruel and inhuman scale. They were not only wholesale assassins, but they also made assassination a law of the Christian church and a condition of salvation."

The Papacy allies itself with strong governments and dictators. It believes in force; always seeks the arm of the State. Great wars have been produced by its intrigue.

11:38 "And a god whom his fathers knew not shalt he honour With gold, and silver, and with precious things, and things desired," margin. See also Isa. 44:9.

Rev. 17:4 "And the woman was arrayed in purple and scarlet colour, and decked with gold and precious stones and pearls. See also Rev. 18:12–19.

11:39 "Thus shall he do within the most strong holds with a strange god, whom he shall acknowledge and increase with glory."

They worship a wafer god—a biscuit—a god such as earlier Christians "knew not."

Also the veneration of Mary. These gods they honour with millions of pounds worth of jewellery. Costly shrines have

		been multiplied in every part of the world.
11:39	"And he shalt cause them to rule over many"	Millions of Rome's devotees are held in bondage by these idols and images.
		Rev. 13:3 "All the world wondered after the beast."
		Rev. 13:8 "All that dwell upon the earth shall worship him."
11:39	"Shall divide the land for gain"	This prophecy concerns the world field: claiming to exercise the vicarship of Jesus Christ over the world, the Papacy believes that countries are subject to its disposal. The Papacy, alone, among all the powers of earth, has claimed the right to divide the world among nations. Observe the following facts:

The Normans went over to Ireland in the reign of Henry II. It was Pope Adrian IV who gave Henry permission to possess the land. That permission is contained in the now famous papal Bull, "Laudabiliter." In that Bull the Pope addresses Henry II in the familiar words, "My well-beloved son in Christ." The Bull contains the following conclusive proof of the accuracy of the prophecy that the Papacy would "divide the land for gain:"

"You have expressed to us your desire to enter the island of Ireland in order to subject its people to law, and to root out from them the weeds of vice, and *your willingness to pay an annual tribute to the blessed Peter of one penny from every house*. . . We, therefore, meeting your pious and laudable desire with due favour and according a gracious assent to your petition, do hereby declare our will and pleasure. . . you shall enter that island. . . ."

Pope Alexander III, who held office in Rome in 1172, at the actual date of the invasion of Ireland by Henry II, solemnly ratified this Bull of his predecessor, Pope Adrian IV, and actually wrote to Henry expressing his confidence that it was the King's desire to "extend the privileges of the church," and "to establish her jurisdiction where at present she has none." The extension of "the privileges of the church" and the establishment of "her jurisdiction" results in the increase of her enormous wealth.

The presumptive power of the Papacy to "divide the land" to its own advantage was brought to view in connection with the discoveries of the new world by Columbus. In his book, *The Prophetic Faith of Our Fathers,* Vol. II, LeRoy E. Froom says:

"The Popes had given Portugal a monopoly on the sea route to India by way of Good Hope. Spain and Portugal, rival sea powers, had found it impossible to traffic with the Far East without violating the papal mandate—until this westward route was proposed, and against which there was no papal edict," pp. 165, 166. This writer continues: "Pope Divides Globe Between Spain and Portugal. The Spanish and Portuguese discoveries offered a wide field for papal extension. However, soon after Christopher Columbus discovered the New World, a hot dispute arose between Spain and Portugal. . . . Ferdinand and Isabella at once dispatched an embassy to Alexander VI for the purpose of ensuring their rights to the new territories, on the principle that Martin V had given to the king of Portugal possession of all lands he might discover between Cape Bojador and the East Indies. . . . In two bulls, of May 4 and 5, 1493, Alexander VI presumed to divide the Western world between Portugal and Spain by a line one hundred leagues west of the Azores, north and south. The possession of the lands discovered, and to be discovered, was assigned to the two countries to be held in perpetuity. . . . Thus half the globe was divided between Spain and Portugal.

"As Peter's successor, the Pope claimed the right to give away the Western continent, a gift that involved an unending right of tenure," pp. 168, 169.

"For gain," or "for a price," margin. Through its false teachings, the Papacy acquires great wealth: "for a price" it can bring forgiveness and comfort to the living; "for a price" it can help the dead who are supposed to be in purgatory. "For a price" it will sprinkle water on infants; "for a price"—according to their ability to pay—Roman Catholics can have a "high" or an ordinary nuptial mass. "For a price" the holy (?) places and things in Jerusalem and Rome can be seen. Bishops, archbishops, etc., are appointed to certain territories in the world and through them the Papacy derives considerable wealth. The Revelator, as well as Daniel, draws attention to this trafficking in connection with the things of salvation—see Rev. 17:4; 18:3, 11–19. The Papacy "for a price" has supported dictators in their covetous ambitions for power. Today, they are bargaining with any force that will operate in any country to bring those countries under their control. "For a price" they lend their aid to ambitious men who desire to rise to power in their respective countries.

By comparing Dan. 11:37–39 and 1 Tim. 4:1–3; 2 Thess. 2:3, 4; Rev. 16:13, 14; etc., we know that Daniel's prophecy (vs. 38, 39) points to the superstitious belief that certain buildings and various countries can be dedicated (Australia has just been dedicated to Mary) to patron and protecting saints as tutelary deities.

Commenting upon Daniel's prophecy and applying it to the Papacy, Matthew Henry's Bible states: "His flatterers call him our Lord god the pope. . . and honours the god of forces, the god Mahuzzim, or strongholds, saints and angels, whom his followers take for their protectors, as the heathen did of old their demons; these they make presidents of several countries, etc. These they honour with vast treasures dedicated to them."

Applying these verses to the papacy, Dr. Thomas says: "He was the god of a new system of idolatry, whose idols were the images of Mahuzzim, or 'the ghosts' of pretended saints and martyrs. . . . Now, to honour a god of guardians with such things, is to enrich the institutions dedicated to the guardian saints. . . . The churches, chapels, and cathedrals are the strongholds, and houses of merchandise, dedicated by the prospering craft to guardian-saints and angels. There are the images and pictures of the saints. They are the saints' houses in which are deposited their shrines; silver, gold, and ivory crucifixes. . . . They are truly Bazaars of spiritual merchandise. . . . But, then, bazaars of priestly wares are distinguished from places of honourable trade, by being dedicated to Mahuzzim. This is a remarkable feature in the prophecy, which finds its counterpart in the dedication of the churches to guardian saints and angels. St. Sophia at Constantinople, St. Peter's at Rome, our Lady's at Paris, St. Paul's at London, and innumerable other bazaars, dedicated to all conceivable kinds of saints, and, lest any should be forgotten, to All Saints, and even to All Souls—are examples in point"—*Elpis Israel*, pp. 365–369.

In his book, *King of the North*, pp. 27, 28, M. C. Wilcox says:

"The whole earth has been divided. Whole countries have been dedicated to patron and protecting saints as tutelary deities. The country has been divided up and cities have been consecrated to different saints as witness in our land—San Francisco, St. Louis, St. Paul, St. Augustine, St. Joseph. And the earth, its countries, its cities, have not only been parcelled out to the saints but to clericals of various ranks, the representatives of the Papacy, and always and ever to the gain of the Papacy."

The translators believed that Dan. 11:36–40 applied to the Papacy for they placed 2 Thess. 2:4 in the margin. Most commentators—

Bengel, Olshausen, Grotius, Bishop Newton, etc.—have agreed that Dan. 11:36 refers to Paul's "man of sin." "Compare," says Alford on 2 Thess. 2:4, "the close parallel in Dan. 11:36, 37."

"This characteristic of impious exaltation is in such striking parallelism with that described by Daniel to the king that shall do according to his will (chap. 11:36), that we can scarcely doubt that the ancient interpreters were right in referring both to the same person—Antichrist"—Ellicott.

After quoting Dan. 11:36, Bishop Newton says:

"From this place, as Jerome asserts, *the Jews as well as the Christians of his time* understood all to be spoken of Antichrist. . . . It is a strong argument in favour of the *Jewish and Christian interpretation,* that St. Paul appears to have understood this passage much in the same manner, because he applies the same expression (2 Thess. 2:3, 4) to 'the Man of Sin, the Son of Perdition, who opposeth and exalteth himself above all that is called God, or that is worshipped; so that he as God, sitteth in the temple of God, showing himself that he is God.' The thread of the prophecy will also conduct us to the same conclusion." *Bishop Newton's Dissertation,* Vol. 2, p. 154.

As did so many Protestant interpreters, William Miller believed these verses described the Papacy. After quoting verse 36 Miller says: "The king here spoken of is the same as Daniel's little horn, which came up among the ten horns. It is the same that blasphemed the God of heaven. It is mystical Babylon (Isa. 14:2–15; Rev. 13:5, 6). The same Paul has described in his epistle, 2 Thess. 2:1–9"—William Miller in *Evidence From Scripture and Prophecy,* pp. 97, 98. After quoting verse 37 Miller continues: "In this passage we have a plain description of the Papacy. . . must convince every one that the description given must apply to the church of Rome, or the Pope, who claims to exercise this great authority by his crazy title to St. Peter's chair." *Ibid.,* p. 98.

By interpreting Dan. 11:36–40 in connection with the French Revolution, and v. 40–45 to Turkey, one has to go contrary to Paul's inspired testimony, and to be heedless of the application made by a great number of God-fearing writers over a long period of time. And where does this interpretation lead? Away from the clear-cut pathway marked by prophecy as it outlines the great controversy between Christ and Satan, and on to a comparatively small track leading into a maze of human speculation. Those who are guided by the Spirit of Prophecy will observe that the Lord's servant gave no sanction to this teaching. "When the books of Daniel and Revelation are better understood" these mis-interpretations in connection with military wars of the vital parts of the prophecies will be applied (as they should be) to the controversy between Christ and Satan. Then, God's people will see from these parts of the prophecies, particularly, "that the connection between God and His people is close and decided" (TM 114). This knowledge, applied to the daily life, will bring about "a great revival" (TM 113).

GUIDANCE FROM THE SPIRIT OF PROPHECY

The Lord's servant, describing the rise of the Papacy, says: "This compromise between paganism and Christianity resulted in the development of the 'man of sin' foretold in prophecy as *opposing and exalting himself above God.* That gigantic system of false religion is a masterpiece of Satan's power—a monument of his efforts to seat himself upon the throne to rule the earth *according to his will. . . .* Satan worked *according to his will*" (GC 50, 51).

It will be observed that the Lord's servant combines the prophecies of Daniel and Paul regarding "the king" who would "*do according to his will*" and "*shall exalt himself.*" In harmony with Paul's application of Daniel's prophecy, God's servant, also, applies it to the Papacy.

In contrast to this positive testimony that Dan. 11:36, 37 applies to the Papacy, the Spirit of Prophecy is entirely silent on the application of those verses to the French Revolution. In *The Great Controversy,* the Lord's servant devoted the whole of chapter 15—pages 265–288—to the French Revolution, commenting at length upon Rev. 11, and referring to passages from the Old Testament. Surely the Spirit of Prophecy would have referred to Dan. 11:36–40 if those verses dealt with the French Revolution! The French Revolution is mentioned in Rev. 11 to explain how the Papacy, described in Rev. 11:1–3 as attacking God's "temple" and "holy city" and His "two witnesses" during the 1260 years of its supremacy, lost its power—by the French people heading the revolt against the church of Rome.

The book of Revelation was given as the complement and supplement of the book of Daniel—what Daniel mentions the Revelator enlarges upon. Daniel has intimated concerning the spiritual temple. The first four chapters of Revelation explain concerning God's spiritual temple in which the seven candlesticks are burning (see Rev. 1:20; 2:1, etc.). Daniel briefly touches upon the break up of the Roman Empire (Dan. 11:30), the Revelator, in the seven trumpets (Rev. 8 and 9) enlarges more fully upon the details omitted in Daniel. In Daniel 7, the Judgment is mentioned; in the seven seals (Rev. 5 to 7)—including the "seal of God"—details are given regarding the Judgment and the Judgment message (compare Dan. 7:10 and Rev. 5:11 ; etc.) Dan. 11:40 does point out the time when "the king of the south," "*Egypt*," pushed "at him," the Papacy. In Rev. 11, where is described the Papal attack upon God's "temple" and "holy city," it also mentions how "the great city, which *spiritually is called* Sodom and *Egypt*" (Rev. 11:8)—the atheistic, immoral French Revolution— was the cause of the Papacy losing its political power to persecute the saints. *If* Dan. 11:36–40 referred to the French Revolution, Daniel's introduction of the subject would be *larger* than the Revelator's *enlargement* of it—which would be contrary to the principle of enlargement shown in regard to the other things introduced by Daniel and enlarged upon by John—a principle which is maintained, also, throughout the prophecies of both Daniel and the Revelation themselves. Their prophecies are so constructed that the succeeding prophecies enlarge upon the essential features mentioned in previous prophecies.

Dan. 11:40 does briefly introduce the French Revolution, but it is enlarged upon in Rev. 11. "The king of the south," who pushed at the Papacy ("him"—"the king of the north"), is interpreted here as those who revolted against the authority of the Papal church at the ending of the time allotted for it to "tread under foot" "the holy city" (see Rev. 11:2, 3).

CHAPTER NINE

THE TERRITORY OF THE KING OF THE NORTH
DEFINED BY SCRIPTURE—NOT BY HISTORY ALONE.

The interpretation of Dan. 11:40–45 does not depend upon ascertaining the precise boundaries of Seleucus Nicator, the founder of the Selucidae, or of his successors. The Lord would not design that the true interpretation of this most important prophecy depend only upon the writings of historians. The student of prophecy is far from despising history or geography for both are useful in the understanding of the prophetic word. But would not the Lord provide in His own inspired Word whatever was necessary for an understanding of this great prophecy? Later, we will point out from God's Word the territory occupied by the king of the north. Men will not be judged by what historians have written, but by the words the Lord has spoken—see John 12:48; Deut. 18:18–20 ; Matt. 4:4.

The endeavour to locate the exact boundaries of the king of the north has occasioned a lot of controversy among prophetic expositors. But all this is unnecessary. However, for a moment, let us consider that the territory of Seleucus Nicator did extend from the Indus to Macedonia, as some have maintained in connection with their belief that Turkey, today, is the modern king of the north. That vast territory is now held by a number of nations. The European portion of Alexander's empire is now divided among Greece, Bulgaria, Roumania, etc. If, through historical uncertainties, it is considered that the government of Seleucus did not extend beyond Asia Minor, we are still faced with the problem that this territory is now held by a number of nations: Persia, Irak, Transjordania, Syria, and the Armenian section of the Russian Soviet Republics. Why should the present Turkish Republic be selected from among these nations as the king of the north? For Turkey to fuse together these separate nations would require that they be submerged by Turkey, but their present independence indicates that they would greatly resent any such attempt by Turkey—*if* she had such a plan—of overcoming their nationalism. Yet surely, if this prophecy be interpreted militarily in reference to

Turkey's future exploits and the setting up of his government in Jerusalem, some such military feat must be accomplished. We are living in a time of extreme nationalism. Even the mighty British Empire has felt obliged to withdraw from countries because of present-day tendencies. If holding the territory of the king of the north determined who is the king of the north, then well might one ask to-day: "Who is the king of the north?" Is it a matter of taking one's choice among a number of nations holding a portion of the northern part of Alexander's empire?

Will Turkey, however, be able to accomplish the tremendous feat of fusing together the broken fragments of the territory which Seleucus either held or is supposed to have held? And then, would Israeli, helped by wealthy Jews in many lands (and many Christians also think that the Jews should inhabit Palestine to fulfill Bible prophecy), be likely to relinquish her firm hold on national status in order to permit the Turks to govern them, or Jerusalem?

However, as will be shown later, the question of the territory of the king of the north must be determined by the Word of God, and not by the speculations of men.

CHAPTER TEN

THE KING OF THE NORTH IS
THE KING OF BABYLON

The term "the king of the north" is a Scriptural one and should be answered from the Scriptures. That "the king of the south" refers to Egypt we are definitely told in Dan. 11:8, 9, for when "the king of the south" returned from his victorious conflict with "the king of the north," he returned "into his own land" and he came "into his own kingdom," which is *distinctly said to be "Egypt."* Thus "the king of the south" is located for us in the Scriptures. See also Dan. 8:9. Now, as the prophecy drops the theme of the king of the south at v. 25 but concludes with the conquests and doom of "the king of the north," he assumes a greater importance for the people of God than "the king of the south." Accordingly, we would expect God would be more certain to inform us from the Scriptures concerning the identity of the king of the north than He would of the king of the south.

The Bible defines its own terms. By comparing Scripture with Scripture, as we are admonished to do, we see that the Bible use of the word "north" is in relation to Babylon and the river Euphrates. The Scriptures emphatically declare: *"The north by the river Euphrates," "in the north country by the river Euphrates"* (Jer. 46:2, 6, 10). In the book of Jeremiah, references are repeatedly made to the coming of the *Babylonians from the north,* the region of the Euphrates, to destroy Jerusalem and to afflict God's professing people. See Jer. 1:13, 14, 15; 4:6; 6:1; 25:9, 26; etc. It was the book of Jeremiah which Daniel studied in connection with his visions (Dan. 9:2). He thus could not be mistaken as to the territory referred to in the term "the king of the north," *for the king of Babylon was declared to be the king of the north.* The Lord had said through Jeremiah: "Behold, I will send and take all the families *of the north,* saith the Lord, and Nebuchadnezzar *the king of Babylon,* My servant, and I will bring them against this land" (Jer. 25:9).

The question as to how far north extended the territory of Seleucus Nicator or his descendants need not be discussed for that has no Scriptural significance. The question, however, is: "Did

Seleucus occupy the territory around Babylon and the Euphrates?"
The decisive answer is "Yes!" As is well known, Alexander the Great
died at Babylon, 328 B.C. When Seleucus Nicator laid the foundations
of the Seleucid kingdom he made Babylon his residence and the
centre of his government. And historians have pointed out that that
empire remained comparatively strong so long as it was governed
from the region of the Euphrates and the Tigris. One of the main
causes of its disintegration was the removal of the centre of its
government to Antioch. Though we would greatly desire to quote a
number of historians, space confines us to a few brief extracts:

"At this division (301 B.C.) *all Syria from the Euphrates to the sea,*
also inland Phrygia, fell to the lot of Seleucus."—*The Roman History,*
quoted in *The Source Book,* p. 211.

"*Babylon was Seleucus's first choice;* and there his court was
held for some years previously to his march against Antigonus."
Later, "He founded, and built with great rapidity, the city of
Seleucia upon the Tigris, at the distance of about forty miles from
Babylon. . . . Seleucus once more transferred the seat of empire. . .
for *almost the western point of his vast territories.* . . Antioch. . . . The
change weakened the ties which bound the empire together. . .
Among the causes which led to the disintegration of the Seleucid
kingdom, there is none that deserves so well to be considered the
main cause as this."—*The Sixth Great Oriental Monarchy,*" George
Rawlinson, M.A., ch. 3, pp. 34, 35.

Concerning the territory of the king of the north, the following brief extract from Myer's *General History* represents many
similar statements made by various historians:

"*Syria, or the kingdom of the Selucidae* (312–65 B.C.).—Under its
first ruler this kingdom comprised nominally almost all the countries of Asia conquered by Alexander, thus stretching from the
Hellespont to the Indus; but in *reality* the monarchy embraced only
Asia Minor, Syria, and the old Assyria and Babylonia. . . but *finally
the country was overrun by the Roman legions and was made a part of
the Roman Republic* (63 B.C.)."

In his *History of Greece,* vol. 4, p. 281, Adolf Holm declares that
ancients regarded the Seleucids "*as in the main having nothing to do
with Asia Minor* at all. . . . *Only Syria and the country to the east of it*
are assigned to the Seleucids."

In Dan. 11:7 the prophecy declares that the king of the south
"shall enter *into the fortress of the king of the north.*" Where was that
"fortress?" We quote from *Daniel and Revelation,* p. 286: "Ptolemy. . .
invaded Syria, slew Laodice, and *proceeded as far as Babylon.* . . took

the city of Seleucia, which was kept for some years afterward by the garrison of the kings of Egypt. *Thus did he enter into the fortress of the king of the north."* (Italics mine.)

Thus the Lord has made doubly sure that by the term, "the king of the north," He means the power possessing territory centred in the region of Babylon and the Euphrates. That the term "the king of the north" applied to the Selucidae because it held territory in the region of Babylonia and Syria will be seen when noticing that the territory of the first king referred to in Dan. 11 as "the king of the north," Antiochus Theos (Dan. 11:6), was practically limited to that region. From Antiochus I to Antiochus III none of the Seleucid kings ruled over Thrace, Macedonia, and most if not all of the provinces of Asia Minor, yet each one is alluded to as "the king of the north."

The last king referred to as "the king of the north," prior to verse 40, is Antiochus III. See Dan. 11:15. Rome, the power that fulfilled Dan. 11:16 and came "against *him*"—the last "king of the north," see v. 15—forced Antiochus III to keep to his territories south of the Taurus mountains. Rollin, in his *Ancient History,* b. 18, c. 1, refers to him as "Antiochus, King of Syria." Later, B.C. 65, Syria was conquered, and added to the Roman empire. The term "the king of the north" is maintained in the prophecy *until his territory is absorbed in the Roman empire.* Then Rome, the second Babylon, becomes the king of the north, and *as such,* stood "in the glorious land, which by his hand was consumed" (v. 16). Subsequent to Rome's conquest of Palestine, B.C. 63, this Roman king of the north attacked the king of the south (Dan. 11:17), and later completely subdued Egypt to his power (v. 25). In the year 30 B.C. Egypt was made a Roman province.

It will be observed that the first time the conquering legions of Rome are represented as moving across the screen of prophecy, they are represented as coming from the north "toward the south" (see Dan. 8:9). As their conquests of "the east" (B.C. 65) and "the pleasant land" (B.C. 63) were prior to Egypt being made a Roman province in B.C. 30, the mention of their move to "the south" before "the east" and "the pleasant land" would serve to indicate their coming from the north.

The prophecy of Dan. 11:15–17 outlines the conquest, first of Syria thus making Rome the king of the north, then Palestine and, continuing on in his conquests, subdues Egypt. Now it will be observed that, in verses 40–45, the king of the north is again pictured as covering by conquests the *same territories as did Rome:* from the north he proceeds in a southerly direction until not only Egypt, but also Libya and Ethiopia are subdued. In other words, the last-day "king of the north"—the Papacy—will do something similar to that done by literal Rome. As we shall show later, the Papacy is represented in earlier parts of the prophecies of Daniel as *repeating in a spiritual sense in relation to the church that which literal Rome did literally in relation to the literal Jews.* However, Papal Rome's power will extend beyond that of pagan Rome's national power—this is the import of the prophecy of Dan. 11:40–45.

It is a custom of Bible writers to bring their readers down to an important part of their prophecy, and then take time to give details by which the power referred to may be identified before proceeding further. Thus, having connected Rome with, and as, the king of the north and "the glorious land," details are then given by which Rome may be definitely identified. Three leading Roman personalities —Julius, Augustus, and Tiberius Caesar—and their outstanding features are mentioned (Dan. 11:17–21), bringing the reader down to the *breaking,* first, of "the Prince of the Covenant" (our Lord, in the nineteenth year of the reign of Tiberius), and, secondly, to the rejected Jewish nation (see v. 22). Regarding the "flood" mentioned in v. 22, compare with Dan. 9:26 and see later references to the river Euphrates "in the *north* country" flooding over its banks as a devastating "flood," and threatening to destroy God's people. Pagan Rome, the king of the north, coming from the region of the Euphrates, flooded the *typical* land of Israel. The Papacy—the spiritual king of the north—situated upon the spiritual Euphrates (Rev. 17:1; Jer. 51:13) will flood across the antitypical land of Israel, and will reach right up to the neck, even to Jerusalem (see Isa. 8:7, 8; Dan. 11:45; etc.), but God's wrath will be poured out upon the flooding of the Euphrates (Rev. 16:12). See further concerning this when we study more closely into Daniel's amazing last prophecy.

Having traced the course of history down to the first coming of Christ and to His death on the cross, and continued on to the end of the Jewish nation, until Rome is completely identified as the king of the north—the "robber" or "breaker" of God's Son, and the Jewish nation—and also the "breaker" of His true people, about which more will be said when dealing with Dan. 11:14 and Dan. 12:7 R. V.—the prophecy then retraces the steps of history to deal with Rome as the king of the north destroying the king of the south. Verse 23 refers to the League made by the Jews with the rising power of Rome (b.c. 161). Here the prophecy goes back to the beginning of the Jews' dealings with Rome and brings down a direct line of events to the final conflict and the second coming of Christ.

Having identified Rome (down to the end of the Jewish nation) as the king of the north, its final attack upon Egypt (in the battle of Actium, B.C. 31) is brought to view in v. 25. Here, the king of the south is again mentioned *as such*—in v. 17 he is not named because the prophet has set out to thoroughly establish Rome as the king of the north before again naming the king of the south. By Rome's attack upon the king of the south—that power that had been *hitherto attacked by the king of the north*—it further suggests that Rome is the king of the north.

The end of literal Rome as the king of the north is intimated in Dan. 11:27: "*the end* shall be at the *time appointed*." Rome was to "forecast his devices from [Newton] the strongholds, even for a time" (11:24), or 360 years. Rome governed from the city of Rome, and in connection with its *final* battle against the forces of *Egypt* it would continue for "a time." Following the battle of Actium, in B.C. 31, Egypt was made a Roman province. Counting 360 years from then brings us to A.D. 330, when Constantine moved the seat of his government from Rome to Constantinople.

Before literal Rome passes completely from the prophecy, mention is again made of the dreadful siege of Jerusalem and the destruction of the Jewish nation (v. 28). The Romans returned "with great riches" from their expedition against Egypt (B.C. 31). After their "exploits" in Judea (A.D. 70) they also returned to their "own land." Verses 29, 30 point to "the end"—"the time appointed"—of the literal Roman power which had centred in Rome. "Constantine's removal of the seat of empire to Constantinople was the signal for the downfall of the empire. Rome then lost its prestige. . . The barbarians of the North soon began their depredations, and extended their conquests till the imperial power of the West expired in A.D. 476.

"This was indeed different from the two former movements brought to view in the prophecy; and to this the fatal step of removing the seat of empire from Rome to Constantinople directly led." *Daniel and Revelation*, p. 317.

Thus from the prophecy drops literal Rome, and from its ancient seat of empire rises the Papacy—the spiritual king of the north. It is to this power that the index finger of prophecy points from the latter part of v. 30 until the end of the chapter (11:45), and also over in chapter 12:7; etc.

CHAPTER ELEVEN

THE KING OF THE NORTH
ATTACKS GOD'S SANCTUARY

The book of Daniel (1:1, 2) commences with the spoliation of God's temple by the Babylonians—the remainder of Daniel deals fully with the temple, and the people of God who are faithful to the teachings centred in that sanctuary, and their enemies who oppose the Lord's sanctuary and its services.

Isaiah said: "Our adversaries have trodden down Thy sanctuary" (Isa. 63:18). "The king of the Chaldees. . . all the vessels of the house of God. . . all these he brought to Babylon. And they burnt the house of God, and brake down the wall of Jerusalem" (2 Chron. 36:17–19). The desolation of the sanctuary by the hand of the Babylonians is the subject of Ps. 74: ". . . All that the enemy hath done wickedly in the sanctuary. Thine enemies roar in the midst of Thy congregations; they set up their ensigns for signs [i.e., within the ruins of the sanctuary]. . . they break down the carved work thereof at once with axes and hammers. They have cast fire into Thy sanctuary, they have defiled by casting down the dwelling place of Thy name to the ground. They said in their hearts, Let us destroy [margin "*break*"—see Dan 11:14; 12:7 R.V.] them together" (vs. 3–8).

God's adversaries made war upon His people and the sanctuary—these two: the people of God and His sanctuary are positively inseparable in the Scriptures. This fact cannot be over emphasized. Without this knowledge the books of Daniel and Revelation cannot be understood aright. Everything in the two books, particularly, revolves around the truths of the sanctuary: the sanctuary in heaven and the spiritual sanctuary on earth. God's adversaries have always sought to "break them together."

Briefly speaking, the sanctuary services were instituted to teach two major truths: (1) the majesty of the Law of God; its holiness and its inviolability: the sinner must die; (2) salvation only through the death of the Saviour. The services of the sanctuary all centred in the Ten Commandments, in the centre of which is the

Sabbath Commandment. In changing the Sabbath, the Papacy struck at the very heart and seal of God's Law, and in doing so struck at the very centre of the entire sanctuary service. This is what the Lord designed to be revealed by the prophecy of Dan. 7. However, the Judgment would sit in the heavenly sanctuary, and upon the earth the spiritual sanctuary would have restored to it the knowledge of the true Sabbath. In Dan. 7, the little horn takes away the Law of God. In the eighth chapter, it takes away the gospel by substituting its own mediatorial system for that which is Christ's. This is the main burden of Dan. 8 and 9.

The prophecy of Dan. 8 and 9 traces the rise of the Roman power: Pagan and Papal. The Lord leads His people to see how ancient Babylon finds its antitype in spiritual Babylon. Literal Rome bridges the history between these two false systems of worship—one centred in literal Babylon on the Euphrates, the other centred in spiritual Babylon situated upon the spiritual river of Euphrates. In Dan. 8 and 9, the invasion of "*the pleasant,*" or "glorious land" (Dan. 8:9) by literal Rome and the destruction of the typical temple, city and nation of Israel, are set forth as a type of the invasion of "the glorious land" by the Papal king of the north (Dan. 11:41) who would do *spiritually in connection with the church*— spiritual Israel, "the temple" of the Lord, "the holy city"—*what literal Rome did literally to the literal nation,* temple and city of Jerusalem. Now Daniel's last prophecy was given to present details of how Rome entered into "the glorious land, which by his hand shall be consumed" (Dan. 11:16): details of how the Papacy arises out of the ruins of the literal Roman empire, and spiritually invades "the glorious land," and attacks God's sanctuary and His Commandment-keeping people.

Dan. 8:10–12 foretold how literal Rome would invade Palestine and slay "the Prince of the host" and destroy the Jewish nation and the sanctuary; these verses also have a double application in regard to the spiritual Romans who would do the same things only *in relation to the church.* "And an host was given him against the daily [Christ's continual sanctuary mediation]" Immediately after these verses, Daniel heard the conversation between our Lord and Gabriel: Gabriel asks, "*How long* shall be the vision concerning the daily, and the transgression of desolation, to give both the sanctuary and the host to be trodden under foot? And He said unto me, Unto two thousand and three score days; then shall the sanctuary be cleansed." That Daniel's last prophecy was given to present details of the vision concerning Christ's continual mediation in the heavenly sanctuary, the substitution of the Papal system of mediation and the treading down of the spiritual sanctuary on earth, is obvious by noting that Dan. 11:31 introduces the Papacy (after the break up of the literal Roman empire, v. 30) by referring back to Dan. 8:11. The principle that nations come into the prophecies when the powers concerned come into contact with God's people applies here: through its counterfeit system of worship it attacks Christ and His people.

Literal Rome ends with Dan. 11:30 and spiritual Rome takes over in Dan. 11:31: "And arms shall stand on his part, and they shall pollute the sanctuary of strength, and shall take away the daily [mediation of Christ], and they shall place the abomination that maketh desolate [the Papal system of mediation that God abominates because of its idolatry and its cruelty to His people]"; Dan. 8:12 says: "And an host was given him against the daily"; Dan. 11:31 says: "And arms shall stand on his part, and they shall pollute the sanctuary of strength, and shall take away the daily." This correct application of Dan. 11:31 in relation to the Papacy and the sanctuary, etc., is further demonstrated by Dan. 12:11, for here we are given the answer relative to the question asked in Dan. 8:13, 14 concerning *"How long"* would the Papal abomination be permitted to *tread "under foot" "the sanctuary and the host?"* We are informed in Dan. 12:11 that "from the time that the daily [mediatorial service of Jesus in the heavenly sanctuary] shall be taken away [as it was by the Papacy in A.D. 508] to set up the abomination that maketh desolate, there shall be one thousand two hundred and ninety days," margin. Commencing with A.D. 508, 1290 years brings us to (1798) the termination of Papal power to persecute God's people.

Now, in Rev. 11:1–3 the persecution of God's people during the Dark Ages is explicitly declared to be an attack upon God's "temple" and "the holy city." That is, the Lord in Rev. 11:1–3 applies *spiritually in connection with the church* that which literal Rome did in connection with the literal city of Jerusalem. Compare Luke 21:24 and Rev. 11:2 and observe that *identical language* is used in both regarding the treading under foot of the city, Jerusalem. The persecution of God's people is clearly outlined in Dan. 11:31–35, this fact is acknowledged by all Seventh-day Adventists. Thus, having introduced in Daniel's last prophecy the Papacy as the power that attacks God's s*piritual* "temple" and "holy city," the prophecy would naturally *continue in this spiritual setting in relation to the church.* Thus Paul applies Dan. 11:36, 37 to the Papacy as if it had succeeded in invading the land of Israel, broken down the walls of "the holy city" and *"sitteth in the temple of God,* showing himself that he is God" (2 Thess. 2:3, 4). Paul also refers to Dan. 11:37 when he says of the Papal system: "Forbidding to marry" (1 Tim. 4:3). The celibacy of the Papal priests and nuns is one of the specifications brought to view in the prophecy of Dan. 11. By its celibacy, the Papacy is able more successfully to enslave both priests and people in their false mediatorial system.

Daniel 7 describes how the Papacy broke into God's spiritual temple and altered the centre of the Ten Commandments—the Sabbath Commandment. Daniel 11 points forward to the time when the final conflict will concern obedience to the Saviour's mediatorial service by strict compliance with the Sabbath Commandment, while the Papacy will seek by all its mighty force to break through the walls of Jerusalem and spoil, as in the Dark Ages, the spiritual "temple" and "the holy city."

The closing verses of Dan. 11 must be understood in the light of the verses that have preceded it: as a description of how Papal Rome will attack the people and sanctuary of God—"the glorious holy mountain"—in the final conflict. Verses 31–35 dealt with the attack by the king of the north upon the spiritual "holy city" (Rev. 11:2); then, he broke into the spiritual temple and city; in the final conflict he will not succeed in repeating what he did then, for he will come to his end, and none shall help him. The church will be delivered for it will be held as a "fortress" "impregnable to the assaults of Satan." See AA 600; DA 323.

CHAPTER TWELVE

OTHER PRINCIPLES OF INTERPRETATION
WHICH SHOULD ALSO BE APPLIED

A nother important principle of interpretation is given by Uriah Smith: "It is a manifest rule of interpretation that we look for nations to be noticed in prophecy when they so far *become connected with the people of God* that mention of them becomes necessary to make the records of sacred history complete."—*Daniel and Revelation*, p. 50.

The application of this principle would mean that Turkey is not the power referred to in Daniel's last prophecy. The power brought to view in Dan. 11:40–45 must be one whose activities *concern the people of God*—such has been Daniel's previous presentations of the work of the Papacy. We are explicitly informed in Dan. 10:14 that Daniel's last prophecy, particularly, was given to show what would "befall" God's people "in the latter days."

Another principle which must be remembered is: "Later revelations are explanations of those given earlier." This principle of "Repeat and Enlarge" operates throughout the Bible. What follows must be considered in the light of what has preceded it. The introduction of a book will often suggest the main features to be considered in the following pages. Thus the sublime declaration at the commencement of the Bible: "In the beginning God created," indicates that throughout the Scriptures we are dealing with an Almighty God; consequently none should be surprised at, or doubt what follows. The second chapter of Genesis enlarges upon the creation of man recorded in the first chapter.

By this principle of "Repeat and Enlarge" we understand why commentators have taught that Daniel's last prophecy is really an enlargement of his earlier prophecies. Uriah Smith believed that the prophecy of Daniel 11 was a commentary on the eighth chapter. In his introduction to the Eleventh chapter of Daniel, he says: "This prophecy, says Bishop Newton, may not improperly be said to be a comment and explanation of the vision of chapter eight; a statement showing clearly he perceived the connection between that vision and the remainder of the book." *Daniel and Revelation,* p. 279.

Daniel's last prophecy was given to him after he had prayed earnestly for three weeks *in order to obtain light on the prophecy recorded in chapters 8 and 9.* As stated by Uriah Smith: "For what purpose did this aged servant of God thus humble himself and afflict his soul? Evidently for the purpose of understanding more fully the divine purpose concerning events that were to befall the church of God in coming time; for the divine messenger sent to instruct him says, "From the first day that thou didst set thine heart to understand," etc. Verse 12. There was then still something which Daniel did not understand, but in reference to which he earnestly desired light. What was it?—It was undoubtedly some part of his last preceding visions; namely, the vision of chapter 9, and through that of the vision of chapter 8, of which chapter 9 was but a further explanation. And as the result of his supplications, he now received more minute information respecting the events included in the great outlines of his former visions." *Daniel and Revelation,* p. 219, 1891 edition.

It is perfectly obvious that as Turkey is not in the slightest degree brought into the prophetic limelight of Daniel's earlier prophecies, it could not possibly be referred to in his last prophecy which was given to explain more fully *what had already been given him.* Throughout the book of Daniel the Lord has given His people a survey of the struggle between the forces of good and evil, and in Daniel's last prophecy He describes the consummation of that conflict. He would not break off just at the climax of His picture of the awful age-long, eternity deciding, world-wide conflict in order to introduce a comparatively small national event, which is entirely foreign to Daniel's prophecies, and also utterly irrelevant to the great controversy. The book of Daniel commences with the historic reference to the invasion of Judea and the overthrow of Jerusalem, the destruction of the temple of God, and the taking of the vessels from the house of God to the house and service of the gods of Babylon. See Dan. 1:1, 2. In harmony with the law of "Repeat and Enlarge," we see that throughout the book of Daniel, Jerusalem, the temple of God, and the "perils, conflicts and *deliverances*" of the people of God are constantly the centre and the circumference. The mention of other powers is merely to point out their enmity to God, His truth, and His people.

The *"final* deliverance of the people of God" (GC 341), to which the prophecies of Daniel and John point, is foreshadowed in the earlier deliverances recorded in the book of Daniel. In his rage at being frustrated of complete dominion, Nebuchadnezzar boastingly said to the three faithful Hebrews, who typify the people of the Third Angel's Message "Who is that God that shall *deliver* you out of my hands?" (Dan. 3:15). The faithful three trusted in the God of Israel to deliver them, and the covenant-keeping God walked with them in the fiery furnace, and *"delivered"* them. The double, or repeated and enlarged, application of this experience refers to the last days, when the people of God—the people of the Third Angel's Message who refuse to bow down to the spiritual image of the beast (Rev. 13, 14, etc.)—will be thrown into times of unparalleled peril; but Jesus, by His angels, will walk with them in the world-wide, spiritual, fiery furnace and will *"deliver"* them from their spiritual Babylonian enemies. Thus we see the connection between the *deliverance* of the three Hebrews, brought to view in Daniel 3, and the *deliverance* of God's world-wide, spiritual Hebrews, mentioned in Dan. 12:1.

In the sixth chapter of Daniel is recorded another instance of deliverance pointing to "the *final* deliverance of the people of God." The plot of Daniel's enemies to persuade the king to pass a Law necessitating a choice between obedience to God's Law or the law of the State, will be repeated and enlarged in its double application when the apostate churches seek government aid to enforce Sunday laws. As the king did not see the subtlety behind the request of Daniel's enemies, so many lawmakers will not discern the cunning behind the appeal to the State to pass laws which will bring spiritual Israel into times of extreme peril. After passing through a night of supreme trust in God, Daniel was *"delivered"* (see Dan. 6:14, 16, 20, 27) from his peril: similarly, spiritual, world-wide Israel, after being plunged into a period of affliction and distress necessitating implicit trust in their God, will be *"delivered"* (Dan. 12:1) at the time of the 6th plague.

As the *deliverances* recorded in the earlier chapters of Daniel point forward to "the *final* deliverance of the people of God," so do the other recorded experiences concerning Jerusalem, its temple, and its people point forward to their repetition and their *"final"* counterpart in the last days. The forces of Babylon that brought peril and disaster to Jerusalem and its temple are repeatedly declared in the book of Jeremiah (a book which Daniel studied in connection with his visions, see Dan. 9:2) to come from "the north." See Jer. 1:13, 14, 15; 4:6; 6:1; 25:9, 26; etc. "The king of the north" refers to the king of spiritual Babylon who, in the last days, will lead his forces in Satan's "final" assault upon the city and people of God.

CHAPTER THIRTEEN

WHO ARE DELIVERED AT THE TIME THE KING OF THE NORTH COMES TO HIS END? LITERAL? OR SPIRITUAL ISRAEL?

The answer to these questions vitally affects and determines our interpretation of the closing verses of Dan. 11. Shall we follow the Futuristic system of interpretation? Or the teaching of the New Testament? Concerning those "delivered" (Dan. 12:1), those who follow the Futuristic system declare: "*Thy people—That is, Daniel's people, the Jews.* Cf. Dan. 9:15, 16, 20, 24; 10:14"—*Scofield's Bible.* Now, it must be admitted that in the verses quoted by Scofield, the terms "thy people" and "my people" undoubtedly refer to the *literal* Jews. How, then, can we apply the same term in Dan. 12:1 to spiritual Israelites? There is not the slightest intimation in the verse itself of any change over from literal, Palestinian Jews to world-wide, spiritual Jews. Surely some principle must operate to determine that a verse which would naturally be understood in the same *literal* sense as previous verses, where the same term is employed, be interpreted in connection with *spiritual* Jews? How do we explain this "spiritual-izing" of the Scriptures? *By principles that are employed throughout the New Testament.*

The New Testament plainly declares that the church is now "the Israel of God" (Gal. 6:16, etc.), and is the inheritor of all the "things" of Israel. The servant of the Lord has declared: "We are numbered with Israel. . . *all* the promises of blessing through obedience, *are for us*"—MH 405. "The Israel of God today. . . the true church." ". . . spiritual Israel—His church on earth." PK 74, 370–372, etc. It cannot be over-emphasized that the New Testament applies the principle that not only Israel typified the church but that *all* associated with Israel in the Old Testament is also to be interpreted in relation to the church. For further consideration of this most important principle of interpretation, the reader is advised to obtain the writer's *Certainty of the Third Angel's Message* and his other publications, such as *The Moral Purpose of Prophecy*.

"The kingdom of God shall be taken from you [*literal* Israel] and given to a nation [*spiritual* Israel] bringing forth the fruits thereof" (Matt. 21:43). To those who bear the "fruit of the Spirit" (Gal. 5:22, 23) in the Lord's vineyard (Matt. 21:33–43; John 15:1–11, etc.) are assured the blessing and protection of God. "Ye [the church] are. . . an holy nation" (1 Pet. 2:9).

The Futuristic system is based upon the denial of this plain, New Testament teaching. *The belief that Turkey comes to his end at Jerusalem* (Dan. 11:46), *with the whole of the interpretation regarding a war between nations in Palestine as "Armageddon," is part of the Futuristic system* and is a contradiction of the principles upon which our message is established. Futurists still build their doctrines upon a belief in a literal, Palestinian fulfillment of the prophecies pertaining to Israel. Thus *Scofield's Bible* (p. 1226) says: "The promise of the kingdom of David and his seed, and described in the prophets (2 Sam. 7:8–17, refs., Zech. 12:8) enters the New Testament absolutely unchanged (Luke 1:31–33)." "Unchanged" so far as the terminology is concerned, but *positively changed regarding the people to whom those prophecies and designations apply.* Here we come to the principle by which Dan. 11:40–45 should be interpreted, to be in harmony with New Testament teachings.

CHAPTER FOURTEEN

THE NEW COVENANT AND THE INTERPRETATION OF THE PROPHECY CONCERNING THE KING OF THE NORTH

Many who preach about the New Covenant do not thoroughly grasp its relationship to the interpretation of prophecy. While believing that the church is the heir to all that anciently belonged to national Israel, many fail to apply this principle when interpreting the prophecies. As indicated in the extract from Scofield given in our previous chapter, expositors of prophecy are led to interpret the prophecies, such as that concerning the king of the north, nationalistically because of the language employed. The language seems to convey that the events portrayed are to be understood in relation to military wars, therefore, they say, they must refer to such. Papists, Futurists, Historicists and others who are looking for the literal, Palestinian fulfillment of such prophecies as Dan. 11:40–45; Ezek. 38; 39; Joel 3; Zech. 14; Isa. 2:1–5; Micah 4:1–8; Rev. 16:12-16, etc. *continue to interpret them according to the Old Covenant.* They fail to heed the principle fully demonstrated in the New Testament that *no matter how nationalistically* a prophecy concerning Israel and her foes may be couched, it is *spiritualized in connection with the church.* The New Covenant is made "with the *house of Israel and the house of Judah*" (Heb. 8:8). The church is now the "*nation*" of Israel (1 Pet. 2:9; Matt. 21:43). The phraseology employed to designate the church is the same as that describing national Israel in the Old Testament. The New Testament *christianizes* Hebrew words and sentiments, and clothes them in an evangelical dress, and consecrates them to Christ and His church. So far as the *words* are concerned, one could believe that it is the same Israel referred to in both the Old and the New Testaments. But that language has to be understood in the light of the many instances in the New Testament where such Old Testament prophecies are spiritualized in connection with the church. Those prophecies which would have had their literal Palestinian fulfillment had the Jews been faithful now have their *spiritual* fulfillment *because the church has taken the place of national Israel.*

The King of the North at Jerusalem

The prophecies of both the Old Testament and the New are given a distinctly Jewish or Palestinian setting. But how could any of the prophecies have been given to the Jews with any but a Jewish or Palestinian setting or background? However, the New Testament clearly interprets these prophecies, in spite of their Palestinian setting, in a spiritual, world-wide sense in relation to the church. The New Testament shows that the things of the Old Covenant have now a world-wide application. The "things" of Israel in the Old Testament are lifted out of their literal setting and employed in a world-wide application in relation to the spiritual kingdom of Jesus Christ. God's last-day Message is based upon the principle that all the "things" of the Old Covenant apply now in an antitypical sense (1 Cor. 10:6, 11, margins; etc.); that the prophecies concerning Israel and her enemies (about which the prophecies cited above pertain) are to be applied in a world-wide sense in relation to the church. Those who expect the literal, Palestinian fulfillment of these and other prophecies take those now world-wide "things" of Christ in the New Covenant, and force them back into a Palestinian setting as under the Old Covenant.

The prophecies cited above do not refer to a military conflict to be waged in Palestine, but are graphic prophetic pictures of the great conflict between the forces of good and evil, couched in a Palestinian setting. As shown later, Daniel's last prophecy was given to reveal the great spiritual conflict. Five times in this prophecy mention is made of "the covenant." The first (Dan. 11:22) points to the crucifixion by the Romans of "the Prince of the covenant." See Dan. 11:22, 28, 30, 32. God's covenant is made with everyone who keeps His Commandments. See Deut. 7:9; 11:13, 14; Jer. 31:33–37. "To a people in whose hearts His Law is written, the favour of God is assured." DA 106. This, of course, is possible only through believing in Christ. Those who join with the Lord in the spiritual conflict are assured of God's blessing and protection. In *Early Writings,* under the chapter heading, "Deliverance of the Saints" (which deliverance of course refers to Dan. 12:1), God's servant says: "It was at midnight that God chose to *deliver* His people. . . [they] hear the *covenant* of peace" that God makes "with those who had kept His Law. . . . God. . . delivered the everlasting *covenant* to His people," p. 285.

Having rejected the provisions of the covenant, the Jewish nation was destroyed by the Romans. In the prophecy of Dan. 11 there occurs a change-over from literal Rome to spiritual Rome (verses 30, 31), as there has been a change-over from the literal Jews to spiritual Israelites. It is significant that when the prophecy passes from literal to spiritual Rome the covenant is referred to three times as "the *holy* covenant"—see Dan. 11:28, 30. There is no change in the covenant, but there is a change from literal to spiritual Israel. Literal Rome co-operated with spiritual Rome in attacking "the holy covenant" between God and His people. Dan. 11:30. From these verses onwards (31–45) the prophecy must be interpreted in relation to spiritual Rome and her spiritual foes—the true Israel of God who are faithful to the covenant, Dan. 11:32. The conflict described in the closing verses of this chapter, *even though couched in a Palestinian setting,* must be interpreted in relation to the spiritual conflict over the Law of God. In Dan. 12:1, those designated "thy people" are spiritual Israelites, even though the wording does not indicate it. In previous parts of Daniel that term applied to literal Israel, but here it refers to spiritual Israelites *because the New Testament has laid down the principle* that all that belonged to national Israel now belongs to the church. Similarly, the New Testament teaching is that the enemies of Israel and all prophecies which have a Palestinian setting (and they all do in principle) have their world-wide fulfillment in relation to the church. This is the principle that must guide in the understanding of Dan. 11:40–45. To interpret these verses in relation to nations engaging in literal conflict in Palestine, is to forget the clear light that shines from the pages of the New Testament and to misinterpret these grand revelations concerning the spiritual conflict as if the Old Covenant concerning national Israel and her "land" (Deut. 15:4; etc.) were still functioning.

One of the noticeable features resultant from interpreting the prophecies according to the New Covenant is that they are greatly enlarged in their meaning and their scope. In the terms of the Old Covenant, their fulfillment would have occurred in the literal land of Israel; in the terms of the New Covenant they are applicable in all the world—the world becomes the spiritual land of Israel, for God's people are found in all the world.

Spiritual things are world-wide in scope, whereas literal things are limited in scope. For example: when a prediction concerning Israel is applied in a literal sense to Palestine, that prophecy is limited to that locality, and it is limited to a particular time. Take the prophecy of Joel 2:23–27 Early and latter rains are predicted to fall upon the "land" of Israel (see v. 18). Futurists apply this passage to literal rains to fall in Palestine. This limits the prophecy in a material sense to both time and place. But the spiritual application is world-wide and, in a limited degree, continuous in time, during this "dispensation of the Holy Spirit."

The King of the North at Jerusalem

Space alone forbids us pointing out that *all* prophecies pertaining to the last days which are interpreted in relation to Palestine, are interpreted according to the terms of the Old Covenant. Satan counterfeits by limiting to Palestine in relation to the Jews that which the Third Angel's Message applies spiritually in all the world.

Applying this principle in our present investigation of the prophecy relating to the king of the north, we would like to point out that verses 36–40 of Dan. 11 are wrongly applied in connection with events covering a few years of the French Revolution. In the New Testament these verses are applied as a description of the Papacy throughout its long history. The same erroneous limitation is also noticeable when Dan. 11:40–45 is interpreted in relation to Turkey and limited to the region around the literal city of Jerusalem; by interpreting these verses in relation to the Papacy and to the great struggle between the forces of good and evil, the events described therein apply in any part of the world where the mark of the beast will be enforced.

CHAPTER FIFTEEN

INTERPRETING DANIEL 11:45 IN
HARMONY WITH THE NEW COVENANT

To national Israel the Lord said: "If ye will obey My voice indeed, and keep My covenant, then ye shall be a peculiar treasure unto Me above all people. . . . And ye shall be unto Me a kingdom of priests, and an holy nation" (Ex. 19:5, 6). Embodied in the Ten Commandments the Lord made the promise: "That thy days may be long *upon the land* which the Lord thy God giveth thee" (Ex. 20:12). "For the Lord shall greatly bless thee i*n the land* which the Lord thy God giveth thee" (Deut. 15:4). "He shall bless thee *in the land* which the Lord thy God giveth thee" (Deut. 28:8; 30:16 ; etc.). "A l*and which the Lord thy God careth for:* the eyes of the Lord thy God are always upon it" (Duet. 11:12). The land promised them is said to be God's land—see Deut. 32:43; Isa. 14:25; Jer. 16:18; Ezek. 38:16; Joel 1:6; 2:18; 3:2. Their sins would cause them to be driven from this land of blessing. Deut. 4:26; 11:17; 28:63; Josh. 23:13, 15, 16; etc. "But if ye turn away, and forsake My statutes and My commandments. . . then will I pluck them up by the roots *out of my land* which I have given them" (2 Chron. 7:19, 20).

Throughout Scripture, the typical character of the promised land (as well as the people, etc.) is revealed. For further consideration of this theme the reader is urged to obtain the writer's *Certainty of the Third Angel's Message.* Not only the sanctuary and its services pointed to something greater, but *"the whole of the previous economy* is affirmed in the New Testament to be *typical"*—see Fairbairn's *Typology of Scripture.* Notice the following extracts from the authoritative work, *The Progress of Doctrine in the New Testament,* by T. D. Bernard, M.S., pp. 128, 129, 222:

". . . the Gospel is *the heir of the Law;* that it *inherits* what the Law had prepared. The Law, on its *national* and ceremonial side, had created a vast and closely woven system of ideas. These were wrought out and exhibited by it in forms according to the flesh—an elect nation. . . a special covenant, a worldly sanctuary, a perpetual service, an anointed priesthood. . . a purchased possession, a holy city, a throne of David, a destiny of dominion. Were these ideas to be lost, and the *language which expressed them* to be dropped when the Gospel came? No! *It was the heir of the Law. . . .* The Gospel claimed them *all*, and developed *in them a value unknown before.* It asserted *itself* as the proper and predestined continuation of the covenant made of God with the fathers, *the real and only fulfillment of all which was typified and prophesied,* presenting the same ideas which had been before embodied in the *narrow* but distinct *limits* of carnal forms, in their *spiritual, universal, and eternal character.* The body of *types* according to *the flesh died with* Christ, and with Christ it arose again a *body of antitypes according to the Spirit.*

". . . The principle that the *same things* which were done under the *old covenant* in the *region of the flesh* are done under the *new covenant* in the *region of the Spirit* opens out in the doctrine of the mediatorial work of Christ in the true tabernacle. . . the sanctification of *believers* as a kingdom of priests and a holy *nation*, and their destined inheritance in a promised land and an holy city of their God. The expansion of these doctrines *fills* and forms *all* the Epistles.

". . . 'Which the Holy Ghost teacheth, comparing spiritual things with spiritual'. . . the interpretation of these words is best derived from the fact everywhere apparent in the Apostle's writings, namely, his *habit* of working out *all* the more recondite and (if I may use the word) scientific parts of the evangelical doctrine *by the aid of the Old Testament, the types, images,* and sentences of which were, we know, in His sight 'spiritual'. . . The appropriation of the *Old Testament words to express the New Testament doctrines* is a part of this elucidation."

Because the correct interpretation of Dan. 11:40–45 depends upon the application of the principle of the typical character in this prophecy (the same typical character applied by Seventh-day Adventists in connection with the previous prophecies of Daniel— Israel, the sanctuary, repairing of the breach in the walls at Jerusalem, the call out of Babylon, etc., etc.), we quote from another well-known authority. In his *Bible Handbook,* pp. 203, 285–292, Dr. Angus says:

" As the future was thus represented in visions, and under a typical dispensation, it can excite no surprise that the whole is often described in *figurative, and allegorical or symbolical* terms. . . . Besides, as everything earthly supplies *images* for describing things spiritual, the law is therefore appropriate as it is necessary.

"In the same way, they speak of His kingdom, *either of grace or glory,* as the highest perfection of the Jewish economy. *It is called*

Jerusalem, or Zion. Isa. 62:1, 6, 7; 60:14–20; Gal. 4:26–28 ; Heb. 12:22. See also Isa. 60:6, 7; 66:23.

"In the same way, the *enemies of the kingdom* of the Messiah are not only *called by the name given to the enemies of the ancient theocracy,* viz., the nations of the Gentiles, but they *often bear the name of some one people,* who, at the time, were peculiarly inimical or powerful. In Isa. 25, they are called by the name of *Moab;* in Isa. 63 and Amos 9:12, by the name of *Edom;* and in Ezek. 38, by the name of *Gog.* . . . Nor need this peculiarity of prophetic language excite surprise. It is *found pervading the whole ancient dispensation."*

Seventh-day Adventist students of Scripture will agree that these statements are a clear summary of the teachings of the whole of the Bible. And by heeding the principle thus expressed there exists among us a unanimity of opinion respecting the interpreta-tion of Daniel's prophecies—until we reach the last verses of Dan. 11. The reason the unity is not maintained in respect to these verses is because those who apply them in relation to Turkey and Pales-tine inconsistently omit the application of the principle of type and antitype which they have maintained throughout the book of Daniel until the last few verses of Daniel 11 are reached! This appears all the more marked when the same principle of the antitype is again applied in the very next verse (Dan. 12:1) regard-ing the term "thy people"—the antitypical, spiritual Israelites! It should not be forgotten that because Israel and their land are antitypically applied here, so must the other nations mentioned in connection with them also have their antitypical characteristics— the king of the north, Egypt, Edom, Moab, the children of Ammon, Ethiopia, Libya.

SEVENTH-DAY ADVENTISTS SHOULD NOT FOLLOW THE FUTURISTIC SYSTEM WHEN INTERPRETING DAN. 11:45.

The Futuristic system, which is Satan's counterfeit of the Third Angel's Message, teaches the strictly *literal* interpretation of the prophecies concerning "Israel and the Holy Land."

Scofield's Bible, p. 918 (notes on Dan. 11), says: "Prophecy does not concern itself with history as such, but only with history as it affects Israel and the Holy Land." Accordingly, Futurism interprets Dan. 11 and other prophecies in relation to Palestine. This is the basic difference between Futurism and our Message. By reading the notes in *Scofield's Bible,* it will be seen that all the prophecies which we as a people apply spiritually or antitypically, in connection with spiritual Israel in all the world, are applied literally in relation to Palestine and the Jews. This fact alone should help Seventh-day Adventists to shun the Futuristic system when interpreting Dan. 11:40-45 ; Joel 3 ; Zech. 14; Ezek. 38; 39; Rev. 16:12-16; etc.

THE SPIRIT OF PROPHECY GUIDES
IN OUR INTERPRETATION

We are given guidance by the Spirit of Prophecy respecting the interpretation of prophecies involving Palestine. In Ezek. 34, under the picture of the flock of God with "one Shepherd over them," Israel feeds "upon the high *mountains of Israel.*"

Commenting upon this chapter, the Lord's servant says: "Christ applied these prophecies to Himself." DA 477. Referring to Ezekiel's prophecies concerning "the *mountains of Israel,* "the Spirit of Prophecy again declares: "Many and wonderful are the promises recorded in Scripture *regarding the church,*" AA 9. "As an earthly shepherd knows his sheep, so does the divine Shepherd know His flock that are *scattered throughout the world.*" DA 479.

Thus the designations, "the land of Israel," "His land," "their land," "the mountains of Israel," etc., now refer to the world-wide kingdom of our Lord, Jesus Christ. In this light we must interpret Dan. 11:45.

CHAPTER SIXTEEN

"THE GLORIOUS HOLY MOUNTAIN"

It would seem incredible if it were necessary to prove to enlightened Seventh-day Adventists that Jerusalem, today, could not possibly be designated by the Lord "the glorious *holy* mountain:" "the *sacred* hill so fair" (*Moffatt's Translation*). The prophecy does not state that Jerusalem which was anciently "holy" will be where the king of the north comes to his end. The prophecy refers to that which will be glorious and holy at the time the king of the north comes to his end. In the prophecy of Dan. 8 and 9, 70 weeks, or 490 years, were allotted to the Jewish nation and to "thy *holy* city" (Dan. 9:24). At the expiration of that period, the Jews and Jerusalem were rejected as the people and city of God.

After God's complete and irretrievable rejection of the literal Jews, the literal city of Jerusalem, and the literal temple, the New Testament writers refer to the church as "Israel" (Gal. 6:16), "the tribes of Israel" (Rev. 7:4–8; 21:12), "Jews" (Rom. 2:28, 29), "the temple" (1 Cor. 3:16, 17; 6:19; 2 Cor. 6:16; Eph. 2:21, 22), "Mt. Zion" (Heb. 12:22; Joel 2:32, compare with Rom. 10:13; Isa. 28:16 with 1 Pet. 2:6–8; Isa. 59:20 with Rom. 11:26; etc.), "Jerusalem" (Heb. 12:22), "the holy city" (Rev. 11:2).

"*The holy mountain*" refers to the dwelling place of God. See Ps. 87:1; Isa. 11:9; 56:7; Joel 3:17; Eph. 2:21; etc. Jerusalem was called "the mountain of the Lord of hosts the holy mountain" *only* when the Lord dwelt "in the midst of Jerusalem." Zech. 8:3. Literal Jerusalem is not now "the glorious holy mountain"—such a designation belongs only to the church. Things are "holy" only when they have a true relationship to the Godhead. God's Presence made "holy" the ground upon which Moses stood (Ex. 3:5). Ancient Israel became "an holy nation" (Ex. 19:6; Lev. 20:26; etc.) when God dwelt among them (Ex. 25:8). But the term "holy people, " applicable to the literal Jews until the time of their rejection, belongs now to spiritual Israel (see Dan. 8:24 and Dan. 12:7) in whose midst the Lord now dwells. See 1 Cor. 3:17; 2 Cor. 6:16; Eph. 2:21; etc. The term, "the holy mountain," belonged to

The King of the North at Jerusalem

Jerusalem so long as God's Presence was there, but that term could not apply to it after God withdrew His Presence and favour when He rejected the Jewish nation as His people. That term now belongs to the church. The church is "an holy nation," "a spiritual house, an holy priesthood" offering "up spiritual sacrifices" upon "Mt. Zion." See 1 Pet. 2:5–9; Rev. 14:1; Ezek. 34:13, 14; 36:1–8; 40 to 48.

In the New Testament, following God's rejection of the Jewish nation, there is a total silence regarding Jerusalem being holy or in any way figuring in God's plan or purposes, and no prophecy made subsequent to that rejection ever employs the points of the compass as if they centred in literal Jerusalem—literal Jerusalem dropped completely out of the prophetic picture. It is contrary to New Testament teachings to apply the term "the glorious holy mountain" (Dan. 11:45) to the rejected city. Roman Catholic reverence for relics lies in their superstitious belief that something holy remains with some place or thing once contacted by a holy person. But unless God's Presence and blessing are ever-present no thing and no place is "holy." To interpret "the glorious holy mountain" (Dan. 11:45) in relation to literal Jerusalem—whether in reference to the Papacy or to Turkey—is merely applying the Futuristic principle of interpretation on a basis level with Roman Catholic reverence for relics.

Just as the term "thy people" employed earlier in the book of Daniel (Dan. 9:15, 16, 20, 24; 10:14) changes automatically from literal to spiritual Israel in Dan. 12:1; just as the "holy people" (Dan. 8:24) changes from literal to spiritual Israel in Dan. 12:7, so the term "*holy mountain*" in Dan. 9:16, 20 changes to the spiritual realm of the church in Dan. 11:45.

CHAPTER SEVENTEEN

JERUSALEM IN THE PROPHECIES:
THE STORM CENTRE OF THE AGES

The Spirit of Prophecy applies prophetic references to Jerusalem in connection with the church. The following are a few examples:

Isa. 4:2, 3: "He that is *left in Zion,* and he that *remaineth in Jerusalem,* shall be called holy, even everyone that is written among *the living in Jerusalem."*

These verses are applied spiritually in relation to the church (GC 485), and with the victory of the remnant people of God over their enemies—5T 475, 476; PK 592.

Zeph. 1:12: "I will *search Jerusalem* with candles, and punish the men that are settled upon their lees."

This verse is quoted spiritually in connection with the church—GC 310; 5T 99, 308; etc.

Zech. 12:8: "In that day shall the Lord defend *the inhabitants of Jerusalem;* and he that is feeble among them at that day shall be as David."

In 5T 81 we read this comment: "The most weak and hesitating in the church, will be as David." See also 6T 42; etc.

Zech. 13:1: "In that day there shall be a fountain opened to the house of David and to *the inhabitants of Jerusalem* for sin and uncleanness."

This verse is employed by God's servant to describe the work of the Gospel (PP 413; PK 695; 6T 227; etc.)—thus *"the inhabitants of Jerusalem"* refers to believers in any part of the world.

Joel 2:1: "Blow ye the trumpet *in Zion,* and sound an alarm in *My holy mountain."*

God's servant applies this in connection with the preaching of God's last-day Message—see GC 310, 311; 8T 195.

The King of the North at Jerusalem

Zech. 14:2, 3, 12-14: "I will *gather all nations against Jerusalem* to battle. . . Then shall the Lord go forth, and fight against those nations. . ." This prophesied gathering of the nations to *fight against Jerusalem* the Lord's servant quotes in GC 657; EW 289 when describing the fate of "those who have professed to be the *spiritual* guardians of the people" (GC 656), but have "fought against Jerusalem"—the true church.

The Spirit of Prophecy, when writing of the last days, never applies a prophecy (no matter how the language would indicate its *literal* fulfillment) in connection with literal Jerusalem, but always in connection with the church.

In the book of Ezekiel, chapters 40 to 48, is a description of a great city and temple "upon a very high mountain" in "the land of Israel" (Ezek. 40:2; etc.). "This is the law of the house; Upon the top of the mountain the whole limit thereof round about shall be *most holy*" (Ezek. 43:12). "Waters issued out from under the threshold of the house *eastward*" (Ezek. 47:1). Concerning the river which emerged from the eastward side of this house on the "very high mountain" in "the land of Israel," the Spirit of Prophecy says: "Wonderful is the work which the Lord designs to accomplish *through His church*. . . A picture of this work is given in Ezekiel's vision of the river of healing. . . (Ezek. 47:8-12)." In 6T 227, 228 God's servant declares that this "mighty river seen in Ezekiel's vision" comes from the fountain opened "to the inhabitants of Jerusalem" (Zech. 13:1), and is being fulfilled in the work being done by God's people today.

That the Christian church is portrayed by the beautiful imagery of the huge temple and city in the "holy oblation" "in the land of Israel," has been expressed by many godly commentators. See *Dr. Clarke's Commentary, Brown's Bible,* etc. The tract of land which was set aside to contain the temple, city, etc., called "the oblation," measured 200 miles around. (See the writer's other publications for further details.) When John pictured the slaughter of those who attacked God's people in the final conflict, he declared that the winepress of God's wrath in which they would be destroyed was "trodden without the city". . . by the space of a thousand and six hundred furlongs" (Rev. 14:20; 19:15). One thousand six hundred furlongs make 200 miles, which is the circuit of the Holy Oblation in which the temple and city were pictured in Ezekiel's vision of the church—"in the land of Israel." "Upon the top of the mountain the whole limit thereof shall be *most holy*." It is called the *"holy* oblation" because *"The Lord is there"* (see Ezek. 43:12; 48:20, 21, 35). The Revelator declares that " Armageddon" "the mountain of slaughter" occurs outside "the holy city"—"the true church." Thus "the glorious holy mountain" (Dan. 11:45) cannot possibly refer to literal Jerusalem, but to the church.

JERUSALEM, THE STORM CENTRE
OF THE GREAT CONTROVERSY

Throughout the Scriptures, the storm centre of the ages is the city of Jerusalem, the name of which means "foundations of *peace;*" Jerusalem, the city of "the Prince of *Peace.*" Jesus likened the church to "a city set on an hill" giving light to "*the world*" (Matt. 5:14). That city is Jerusalem built on Mt. Zion: "Jerusalem. . . is the city of the great King" (Matt. 5:35). To correctly understand all the prophecies depicting the spiritual conflict, *Jerusalem must be interpreted as the centre of the battle between good and evil.* In the Old Testament, Jerusalem was the literal centre of national Israel, and many of Israel's national enemies came against Jerusalem—the city of "peace." Though foes were without, peace reigned within the city when Israel was faithful. In this we see typified the church as a whole, and also each individual. Through their allegiance to God, the church and individual Christians become the centre of attack by foes who are stirred to "war" against the Holy Son of God within. But, while enemies gather outside the walls of "the holy city" (Rev. 11:2, etc.), the heart is at peace with God. After the millennium, Jerusalem—"the New Jerusalem"—will still be the centre within which "the Prince of Peace" reigns, but enemies, bent on "war," will literally gather outside.

As the writer has fully demonstrated in his *Certainty of the Third Angel's Message,* the principle upon which the book of Revelation is based is that of the triple application of the things of Israel: (1) Historic events of ancient Israel; (2) their *spiritual* application in this "dispensation of the Holy Spirit;" (3) a literal application in reference to the eternal kingdom. Old Testament historical or prophetical references to attacks upon Jerusalem are *spiritualized in the New Testament sermons and prophecies* in relation to the church. Enemies of the people of God who literally gathered around and attacked ancient Israel's literal city of "peace" are brought into the spiritual imagery of the Revelation as types of the enemies who gather around to attack the spiritual city of spiritual Israel. The Revelator carries this representation through until the end of the 1,000 years: then, *all* the literal enemies of ancient Israel and *all* the enemies of the church will literally gather around the literal city in which reigns the visible Son of God, the Prince of Peace, the Destroyer of the evil which makes "war" on Him, and on His people.

The King of the North at Jerusalem

Prophecies depicting the final conflict over the Law of God—such as Dan. 11:40-45; Joel 3; Zech. 14 ; Ezek. 38; 39; Rev. 16:12-16—employ the same phraseology *as if Israel still dwells* in "the Holy Land." The language is the same, but its application is different: it does not refer to national, but to spiritual Israel; the land is not the literal but the spiritual land of Israel; the enemies do not literally gather against the literal city of Jerusalem, but they are represented as if they did—for Jerusalem is the type of the church. These same prophecies apply both before and after the millennium. They may be summarized as follows: Before the millennium, Satan attacks Christ in His church, the *spiritual* Jerusalem; after the millennium, Satan attacks Christ and His church within the *literal* Jerusalem: before the millennium, the "war" is a *spiritual uniting* to attack the spiritual centre; after the millennium, it will be a *literal gathering* and a literal attack upon the literal centre—the holy city.

The "war," or "battle," which the Revelator describes from its commencement in heaven (Rev. 12:7) until its close (Rev. 20:8), is *"the* war" between Christ and Satan depicted in *"The* Conflict of the Ages" series of the Spirit of Prophecy. The Bible and the Spirit of Prophecy teach that *the* "battle" (Rev. 20:8) after the millennium is the *same* "battle," or "war" (Rev. 12:17; 16:14; 17:14; 19:11-21) as before the millennium. Rev. 16:14 calls it "THE battle," and some authorities state that the original of Rev. 19:19 and 20:8 refers to "THE battle." Moffatt's Translation of Rev. 20:8 terms it "THE fray." Futurism, which basically is *Satan's attack upon the Law of God,* depicts these prophecies concerning *the* great controversy, in relation to military wars to be fought in Palestine. Seventh-day Adventists who proclaim these prophecies in this military sense are assisting the designs of Satan.

The final conflict will be waged *"without* the city" (Rev. 14:20). "The fugitives whom the Eternal calls shall be i*nside* Jerusalem" (*Moffatt's Trans.* Joel 2:32). This prophecy declares that *"deliverance"* will come to *"the remnant" "in Mount Zion and in Jerusalem."* Joel 3 is the continuation of the same prophecy: the gathering of the nations around Jerusalem and the "deliverance" of Israel "inside Jerusalem" can refer only to the victory of God's Commandment-keeping "remnant" against whom Satan is to make "war" in the last days (Rev. 12:17). This is precisely what is taught in the prophecy concerning the king of the north who will encamp around Jerusalem (Dan. 11:45) with the intentions of destroying it, when he comes to his end by the intervention of the Lord on behalf of His people.

CHAPTER EIGHTEEN

NORTH, SOUTH, EAST AND EGYPT IN DAN. 11:40-45

Having shown that "the glorious holy mountain" refers to the church, it naturally follows that whatever else is mentioned in the prophecy must be interpreted in harmony with that fact. It is impossible to have a literal north, south and east in the usual sense literally based upon a spiritual mount or city. As Jerusalem, the church, is world-wide so the geographical points of the compass must be interpreted accordingly. The literal points of the compass mentioned in the prophecies concerning Israel and her enemies are now spiritually applied in relation to spiritual Israel, "the holy city." See Isa. 11:12-14; 60:1-12 ; Ezek. 38:12, 5, 6; 39:2, 7; 47:1-8; Joel 3:2, 9-14, 17, 21; Jer. 3:17; Isa. 54:15, 17; Rev. 19:19; 17:13, 14; 16:14; Eph. 2:21, 22; etc.

The loud cry from heaven (Rev. 18:1, 2) is based upon the coming of the Lord to the "east" gate of the temple "upon a very high mountain" "in the land of Israel" (Ezek. 40:2; 43:12): "And the glory of the God of Israel came from the way of the *east*. . . and the earth shined with His glory. . . And the glory of the Lord came into the house by the way of the gate whose prospect is toward the *east*" (Ezek. 43:1-4). The Revelator's application of this shows that when "east" is employed literally in relation to the church, it refers to the east of the whole world. When Jesus comes He will be seen coming in the literal eastern heavens. See GC 640; EW 15. The "east" mentioned in Rev. 7:2 and 16:12, also Matt. 24:27; etc., refers to the "east" of the whole world. Thus, from the application made by the New Testament of Old Testament prophecies mentioning the east of "the mountains of Israel," we know that north, south and east of Dan. 11:40-45 do not have any literal significance in relation to literal Jerusalem. After the rejection of the Jewish nation no prophet of God ever mentioned literal Jerusalem as the centre from which emanated the points of the compass. The church (having taken the place of the literal Jews) is depicted *as if it were Israel still dwelling in "the Holy Land."* The teaching that the king of the north refers to Turkey and that Gog coming from "the north parts" (Ezek. 39:2) refers to Russia, completely ignores the New Testament which applies those prophecies in relation to the church—and NOT in relation to the literal Jerusalem.

As another example of how literal directions of the compass mentioned in the Old Testament lose their relation to literal Jerusalem when referred to in the Revelation, observe Zech. 6:1-15 and compare with Rev. 6:1-8. The four coloured horses of Zechariah's prophecy do their appointed work in connection with the deliverance of God's people from ancient Babylon and their call back to Jerusalem to rebuild the temple and city. From Babylon in "the north" to Egypt in "the south," God's people were given the call to come to "build in the temple of the Lord." When the Revelator employs these coloured horses to describe the conflicts and progress of the church (Rev. 6) in building the spiritual temple while fighting against the forces of Babylon and of the world, he does not mention anything concerning "north" or "south."

Prophecies depicting a gathering of God's people from *all directions of the compass to Jerusalem,* are always employed in the Spirit of Prophecy in a spiritual sense in relation to the church. See Isa. 11:11, 12; 60:1-11; etc., and notice the application in *The Acts of the Apostles,* p. 595 ; *Early Writings,* pp. 74-76; etc.

Egypt, the literal king of the south, in the early parts of Dan. 11, is mentioned in Rev. 11:8 in a spiritual sense. *Jerusalem,* which also comes into the study of Dan. 11, is likewise mentioned in Rev. 11:2 in a *spiritual* sense, for here "the true church" is said to be "the holy city." As shown elsewhere, the Revelator in chapter 11 of his book refers to Dan. 11: Egypt, the king of the south, the Papacy, the king of the north who attacks "the holy city," and the church, "the holy city." Egypt, the king of the south who pushes at the Papacy (see Dan. 11:40) is mentioned in Rev. 11:8 in connection with the revolutionaries who deluged France with blood at the time of the French Revolution. They ascended "out of the bottomless pit" (Rev. 11:7): they came from "beneath." See Prov. 15:24; Isa. 14:9; John 8:23. Commenting upon the power referred to as being *"spiritually Egypt,"* and applying it to the French atheistic revolutionaries, the Spirit of Prophecy says: "This is atheism; and the nation represented by Egypt would give voice to a similar denial of the claims of the living God." GC 269. The French Revolution was really a revolt against the authority of the Papal church, which suffered severely at the hands of the revolutionaries. Thus did "the king of the south *push* at him" (the Papacy) "at the time of the end." Thus the Papacy, whose persecutions of the church are mentioned in Dan. 11:32-36 and which are depicted in Rev. 11:2 as an attack upon "the holy city," and the king of the south that pushes at the king of the north, *are each mentioned in both Dan. 11 and Rev. 11*. From Rev. 11 we therefore see that the prophecy of Dan. 11 is interpreted spiritually in relation to the church.

Lamenting over the worldly state of the church, God's servant says: "The church has turned back from following Christ her Leader and is steadily retreating toward Egypt." 5T 217.

As shown elsewhere, Babylon is said to be "north" of Jerusalem. Babylon's destruction would be brought about by nations to the north and to the east. See Jer. 50:9 ; Isa. 41:2, 25; 46:11; etc. In harmony with the type, spiritual Babylon will be destroyed by heavenly powers coming from the north and the east. God's throne is said to be in the north. See Psalm 48:2; Ezek. 1:4; Isa. 14:13, 14; etc. However, whenever heavenly beings or messengers come down to visit the earth, because of the rotation of the earth upon its axis from west to east, they appear as if coming over the eastern horizon. Thus God's last-day Message, from the throne of God (Rev. 5:1; etc.), comes from the east (Rev. 7:2). The loud cry (based upon Ezek. 43:1-4, where the glory of the God of Israel is said to be manifested at the *eastern* gate of the temple) is "the tidings" which come "out of the east and out of the north" that "*trouble* him," Babylon, "the king of the north."

Referring to the completion of the work of God on earth, the Lord's servant says: "I was pointed down to the time when the third angel's message was closing. The power of God had rested upon His people. . . The last great warning had been sounded everywhere, and it had *stirred up and enraged* the, inhabitants of the earth who would not receive the message." EW 279.

The loud cry will be given with such mighty power that the king of the north will become greatly *troubled* thereby; "*therefore* he shall go forth with great fury to destroy, and utterly to make away many" (Dan. 11:44), and to accomplish his designs he encamps about the spiritual "holy city," but the Lord intervenes to deliver His people—this is the teaching of Dan. 11:45; 12:1.

CHAPTER NINETEEN

"THESE SHALL ESCAPE OUT OF HIS HAND, EVEN EDOM, AND MOAB" (DAN. 11:41)

In harmony with the fact that the term "thy people" in Dan. 12:1 must be interpreted *spiritually,* according to New Testament teaching, so nations mentioned in prophecies concerning "Israel" must also be applied spiritually. Thus Edom in Dan. 11:41 is not to be understood as referring to literal Edomites—of which there are none in the world today! Observe the New Testament interpretation of the prophecy of Amos 9:11, 12 concerning Edom. Israel was to "possess the remnant of *Edom,* and of all the heathen," or "Gentiles." Paul, Barnabas and Peter each came to the church council held at Jerusalem to give their testimony of the wonderful way the Lord was working through them in winning Gentiles to the Lord. After summarizing Peter's testimony very briefly, James quotes this prophecy of Amos 9:11, 12 to show that this prophecy was meeting its fulfillment in the winning of souls from *"among the Gentiles."* In the prophecy of Amos we read: "That they [Israel] may possess the remnant of *Edom."* James reads it as: "That the residue of men might seek after the Lord, and all the Gentiles" (Acts 15:7, 12-17).

The apparently literal, or geographical, sense of the prophecy of Amos is thus applied in a general sense in relation to the spiritual victories of the church in the conversion of the Gentiles. Anciently, the Edomites were the enemies of God's people, and at every occasion sought to harm the people of God. *They assisted the Babylonians in the destruction of Jerusalem.* In reference to this, the Psalmist says: "Remember, O Lord, *the children of Edom* in the day of Jerusalem; who said, Rase it, rase it, even to the foundation thereof" (Ps. 137:7). In a number of places in Scripture the Edomites are employed symbolically as the enemies of God's people—see Isa. 34; 63:1-6; etc. In these passages the Edomites, or Idumeans, are represented as being in rebellion against God: they are the representatives of those who are hardened against the truth and God's people. In the hard times when the early church struggled against formidable odds, the winning of souls was like that of persuading Edomites to become persecuted Israelites. Even such usually hard people, according to Dan. 11:41, will be won when the mighty power of the loud cry strengthens them to escape from the hands of the Papacy.

In Isa. 11:11-16 we have a parallel prophecy to that of Dan. 11:41-44. Isaiah's prophecy declares: "The Lord shall set His hand again the second time to recover the *remnant of His people,* which shall be left, from Assyria, and from Egypt [note Dan. 11:42, 43], and from Pathros, and from Cush, and from Elam, and from Shinar, and from Hamath, and from the islands of the sea. And He shall *assemble* the outcasts of Israel, and gather together the dispersed of Judah from the comers of the earth. . . They [God's people] shall lay their hands upon *Edom and Moab; and the children of Ammon* shall *obey* them." Notice that these are the very people mentioned in the prophecy concerning the activities of the king of the north—Egypt, Moab, Edom, and the children of Ammon. In Dan. 11:41 we read: "But these shall escape out of his hand [the hand of the king of the north], even *Edom, and Moab, and the chief of the children of Ammon."* These are the very ones mentioned in the prophecy of Isa. 11 as obeying "the remnant of His [God's] people." That is, through heeding God's last-day message of salvation, they "escape out of his hand" and take their stand with the people of God *"inside* Jerusalem," "the holy city."

In EW 74-76, God's servant makes a *spiritual* application of the prophecy of Isa. 11:11-16. As the Lord's servant has thus spiritualized *the apparently literal* prophecy of Isa. 11:11-16 in relation to the conflict between the forces of good and evil, the *same people* mentioned in the *same way* in the prophecy of Dan. 11 cannot logically be interpreted in any other way than in connection with the *spiritual* conflict—and *not* in connection with military exploits interpreted in relation to literal Jerusalem.

Commenting upon the prophecy found in Num. 24:17, the Spirit of Prophecy teaches that "Moab and. . . all the children of Sheth" represent "the enemies of God." PP 451. Today, and particularly in the loud cry, from among the ranks of God's enemies, souls are being saved, and will yet be saved, to take their stand with God's people. See EW pp. 277-279. Thus will "these escape out of his hand"—the hand of the Papacy.

CHAPTER TWENTY

THE NEW TESTAMENT DETERMINES THE CHANGE FROM THE LITERAL TO THE SPIRITUAL IN OLD TESTAMENT PROPHECIES

A study of the New Testament—of sermons recorded therein or of epistles, etc., written after Pentecost—will clearly reveal the fact that the disciples *spiritualized* Old Testament prophecies concerning Israel and her enemies. It was this *"better understanding"* of the prophecies of Daniel and other Old Testament prophecies that filled them with a zeal that envisioned them to preach Christ to hostile people, that caused them to face martyrdom with fortitude. The same realization of the spiritual meaning of the prophecies concerning the final conflict will also stir the people of God today, and will bring about that *"great revival"* which the Lord's servant says will follow from "a better understanding of the books of Daniel and Revelation."

The New Testament makes it plain that the prophecies concerning the reign of David's Son were being fulfilled subsequent to His death and resurrection (see Acts 2:29, 32; 13:22-24, 32-34; Rom. 1:3, 4; 2 Tim. 2:8). Paul preached the kingdom of God and of Christ as a then reality, into which every believer of the gospel was, and is, instantly translated (Col. 1:12, 13; 1 Cor. 15:1, 2; Acts 20:24, 25, etc.) God has "raised unto Israel a Saviour, Jesus" (Acts 13:22, 23; Luke 1:68-70; 2:10, 11, 30-32; Acts 5:30, 31). By the work of the Holy Spirit in Messiah's spiritual kingdom of grace, Christ is *now* saving, redeeming Israel out of "all people." That salvation is *"in* Zion" (Joel 2:32; Rom. 11:26; 9:23-33; 1 Pet. 2:4-7), in the church, where Jesus reigns.

When the disciples, who were still thinking of the immediate *literal Palestinian* fulfillment of the Old Testament kingdom prophecies, asked: "Lord, wilt Thou at this time restore again the kingdom to Israel? He said unto them, It is not for you to know the times or the seasons. . . BUT *ye shall receive power,* after that the Holy Ghost is come upon you" (Acts 1:6-8). Prophecies concerning the Messiah's kingdom are now being fulfilled through the power of the Holy Ghost. "For the kingdom of God is not in word, but in power" (1 Cor. 4:20).

Jesus is *now* reigning! The prophecies concerning His kingdom of grace are *now* being fulfilled ! This was the thrilling burden of the apostles' preaching after the descent of the Holy Spirit on Pentecost! It was this recognition of the fulfillment of the kingdom prophecies in relation to the church that gave power to their preaching, and which also aroused the anger of the Jews against them. That which the Jews regarded as being wholly *future,* and to be fulfilled *literally* in connection with national Israel, the apostles preached as being fulfilled in the work of preaching the gospel. Today, Christendom has been led so far astray in its understanding of the prophecies that it takes the same view of those prophecies as did the Jews: *the literal, Palestinian fulfillment in relation to the Jews.* When the people of God, like the early disciples, seek God more earnestly in prayer and study and the Holy Spirit is poured out more fully upon them, they, like the disciples, will emphasize more the spiritual interpretation of those prophecies which are so popularly applied literally in relation to Palestine. As such preaching angered the Jews, so such preaching today, backed home by the power of the Holy Spirit, will also create antagonism.

On the day of Pentecost, the inspired Peter declared that Jesus was raised to sit upon a throne; that He was "both *Lord* and *Christ*" (Acts. 2:30-36). Peter's sermon was very largely made up of quotations from the Old Testament. The first of these is a long quotation from Joel 2:28-32. Peter also quoted from Ps. 110:1. The remarkable feature about this Spirit-filled address which brought such results in soul-saving was Peter's *spiritualizing* of these prophecies in relation to the work of the church. Peter quotes Joel's prophecy addressed to ancient Israel and applies them to all those who believe in Jesus as "both *Lord* and Christ:" "*all* flesh," "*whosoever* shall call on the name of the Lord shall be saved." In Acts 2:33, Peter declares that the outpouring of the Spirit predicted by Joel was a demonstration of the fact that Christ had *already* received and *was* exercising *His royal authority.* The King is *now* exercising His sovereign power. Note this significance in such verses as Acts 3:16; 4:10, 30; 5:31; etc.

Peter's quotation from Joel 2:32 (see Acts 2:21 and compare with Joel 2:32) shows that from the time of Pentecost Old Testament prophecies concerning Zion, Jerusalem, the land of Israel, etc., were interpreted as being fulfilled *spiritually* in connection with the work of Christ in preaching the gospel. From the time of Pentecost the Holy Spirit has inspired the writers of Scripture to present a *spiritual, world-wide* application of the Old Testament prophecies concerning Israel, the land of Israel, Jerusalem, etc.

In other publications the writer has fully demonstrated this principle. Space confines us in this book particularly to the book of Daniel, though we turn for corroboration to the Saviour's prophecy (Matt. 24; Luke 21), and the book of Revelation.

The book of Daniel commences with reference to the Babylonian invasion of Judea, the destruction of Jerusalem and the temple of God, and the taking of the vessels from the house of God to the house and service of the gods of Babylon. In the light from the New Testament we see the principle of understanding the book of Daniel: the principle of type and antitype. *When passing over into the Christian era there is an automatic transition* from literal to spiritual Babylon; from literal to spiritual Jerusalem; from the literal lands of Israel and Babylon to their spiritual antitypes. What literal Babylon did to the literal Jews, Jerusalem and the temple, is also done, in a *spiritual* sense, by spiritual Babylon in her spiritual "war" against spiritual Israel.

In the prophecy of Daniel Two, the transition from the literal to the spiritual may be seen. Beginning with Nebuchadnezzar, the king of *literal* Babylon, the prophecy continues down to the time of spiritual Babylon, centred in Europe—the cradle of nominal Christianity. The position of absolute monarch occupied by the king of literal Babylon (Dan. 2:38) will be duplicated, in a spiritual sense, when the Papacy, through the enforcement of her "Sunday" by the nations of Christendom, will be exalted among the people and shall say (in the pride of Nebuchadnezzar who boasted of the "*great* Babylon" he had built—see Dan. 4:30) "I sit a queen, and am no widow, and shall see no sorrow" (Rev. 18:7). The expression "*Great* Babylon," used by Nebuchadnezzar, forms the basis of the Revelator's description of spiritual Babylon—see Rev. 14:8; 16:19; 17:18; 18:2, 10, 16, 18; 19:2, 3.

In chapter eight, we have already shown the transition from the literal to the spiritual in the experiences of the three Hebrews, and of Daniel in his non-compliance with the Law of the State.

Chapter 7 of Daniel commences with literal Babylon, and passes on to spiritual Babylon, headed by the little horn. In describing the beast (Rev. 13:2) representing the Papacy, John passes from the leopard (Grecia) and the bear (Medo-Persia) to the lion (Babylon). See Rev. 13:2 and compare with Dan. 7. By this transition from *literal to spiritual Babylon,* the Holy Spirit illustrates the principle to be followed in the study of the book of Daniel.

The same transition is also seen in relation to the two phases of Rome. Verses 23-25 of Dan. 8 uses the same words to picture both pagan and papal Rome. What Rome did nationally, spiritual Rome did, and does, in a *spiritual* sense. The words "shall prosper, and practise, and shall *destroy the mighty and the holy people*" fit both literal and spiritual Rome. Pagan Rome invaded the *typical* land, and destroyed many Jews, their city and temple. Spiritual Rome invaded the *spiritual* land of Israel, and destroyed millions of the members of spiritual Israel, and greatly damaged the spiritual "Holy City" (Rev. 11:2). The transition from literal to spiritual Rome automatically takes place, in harmony with the New Testament principle. That papal Rome, in addition to pagan Rome, is described in Dan. 8:24 is evident from the fact that, in Dan. 12:7, this work of destroying "the holy people" is said to occur during the 1260 years of Papal supremacy. When Jesus, in Matt. 24, quotes from the prophecy of Daniel regarding the coming of "the abomination of desolation"—the Roman armies (Luke 21:20; GC 21, 26)—to "destroy the city and the sanctuary" (Dan. 9:26, 27; Luke 21:20), and then passes, *without a break in His sermon,* to depict the destruction of the saints during the Dark Ages (Matt. 24:15-20 and notice 21, 22), He follows the principle employed in the book of Daniel. The "breaking in pieces" (Dan. 12:7, R.V.) and the scattering of the Jewish nation, referred to by Jesus in Luke 21:24; Matt. 21:43, 44, etc., was the literal fulfillment: but in the Dark Ages occurred the spiritual fulfillment, when *papal Rome attacked the spiritual city and temple*—His church.

The same principle of the transition from the literal and local to the spiritual and world-wide is seen in the prophecy of the 2,300 days. They commence (457 B.C.) with the decree for the return of the Jews from Babylon "to restore and to build Jerusalem" (see Dan. 9:25; Ezra 7, etc.)—to "repair" (see Neh. 3; Isa. 58:12, 13) the damage done by the Babylonians. The ending of the 2,300 days brings us to the time spiritual Israel comes out of Babylon (Rev. 18:4) to "restore all things" (Matt. 17:11; Mal. 4:5, 6)—the true temple service (Rev. 11:1, 2)—and to "repair" the breach (Isa. 58:12, 13).

As would naturally be expected, the same principle is maintained in Daniel's last prophecy. From the last hours of literal Babylon, recorded in Dan. 5, we pass on to the last hours of spiritual Babylon (Dan. 11:45). Literal Babylon was "weighed in the balances and found wanting" (Dan. 5:27); the decisions of God's Judgment were pronounced and disaster speedily followed. At the conclusion of Daniel's last prophecy, we are also brought to the time when God's Judgment is pronounced upon modern Babylon: it, too, is "weighed in the balances and found wanting;" Christ completes His mediatorial work, probation closes and the seven last plagues speedily fall upon the persecutors of God's people (Dan. 12:1).

While the literal Babylonians were praising their gods, Cyrus and his army—"the kings of the east" (Isa. 41:2, 25 ; 46:11; Jer. 51:11, 28) with their allies of the north (Jer. 50:41; 51:27, 28)—having "dried up" the waters of the Euphrates (Isa. 44:27; Jer. 50:38; etc.)—entered and overthew the city of Babylon. Daniel's last prophecy (10 to 12) commences with Cyrus (Dan. 10:1)—Israel's deliverer, and the destroyer of her Babylonian oppressors (see Jer. 50:33, 34; Isa. 44:28; 45:1, 13; etc.). Again we see the transition from the events associated with the downfall of literal Babylon to the world-wide events associated with the downfall of modern Babylon (Dan. 11:45; 12:1). Cyrus, whose name meant "the sun," is brought to view in the Scriptures as a type of Jesus "the Sun of Righteousness" (Mal. 4:2). The "double" application of the overthrow of Babylon by Cyrus refers to the coming of Jesus, the Almighty "Cyrus," the Shepherd-King (see regarding Cyrus in Isa. 44:28), the Lord's Anointed (see also Isa. 45:1), the Deliverer of Israel (Dan. 12:1; Isa. 45:13), the One Who bids His people go free (Luke 4:18) to worship their God (Isa. 44:28; 2 Chron. 36:22, 23; Ezra 1:1-8).

Daniel 11:44, 45; 12:1 points forward to the time when spiritual Babylon will oppress spiritual Israel, and the waters of the Euphrates upon which Babylon, the great Whore, sits (Rev. 17:1, 15; Jer. 51:13), will be "dried up" (Rev. 16:12). The 6th plague falls upon the "multitudes" (Rev. 17:15)—the waters which support the great spiritual Babylonian Whore, and which are about to slay the saints at the behest of Babylon. In the chapter (40), "God's People Delivered," the Lord's servant says: "The people of God. . . still plead for divine protection, while in every quarter companies of armed men, urged on by hosts of evil angels, are preparing for the work of death. It is now, in the hour of utmost extremity, that the God of Israel will interpose for the *deliverance* [i.e., Dan. 12:1] of His chosen. . . The angry *multitudes* are suddenly arrested" (GC 635, 636). Thus God's servant connects up the *deliverance* (Dan. 12:1) of God's people with the outpouring of the 6th plague. The 6th plague is poured out upon the Babylonian "multitudes" who are seeking to slay the saints. When the mighty demonstrations of God's power are revealed on behalf of His people, the "multitudes" turn and rend their spiritual advisors—thus the waters of the Babylonian Euphrates will no longer be Babylon's bulwark and glory, but serve to bring about her destruction.

The Lord will come to "deliver" His people from their Babylonian oppressors, and take them to worship God in their native land—the eternal Canaan (Dan. 12:13). It was to reveal these glorious truths that God gave Daniel his last prophecy. There is not the slightest suggestion of a great battle to be fought among the nations as the climax of Daniel's prophecies. By this teaching Satan seeks to deflect God's people from the thrilling truths which are fully enlarged upon in the Spirit of Prophecy. The main burden of the books of Daniel and Revelation concerns the "dangers, con-flicts, and *final deliverance* of the people of God." It was to obtain light upon this important theme that caused Daniel to fast and pray for three weeks. This was the theme in the prophecies of chapters 7, 8, 9. There still remained some light to be given on "the *final* deliverance" of God's people. To make this clear, the Lord gave Daniel his last prophecy. The belief in a military, or Palestinian, "Armageddon" is Satan's smoke screen behind which he hides the light God has given on the deliverance of God's people from their Babylonian persecutors.

CHAPTER TWENTY -ONE

THE ENFORCEMENT OF SUNDAY LAWS
WILL FULFILL DANIEL 11:45

Daniel 11:45; 12:1 teach that the Papacy will employ all of its powers to destroy "the holy city," the church of the living God, but that the Lord will protect His people and destroy their enemies. This is the teaching of the book of Daniel, the Lord in His second advent sermon, and also in the book of Revelation; it is also the teaching of the Spirit of Prophecy. In *Testimonies*, Vol. 5, pp. 451, 452 we read:

"As the approach of the Roman armies was a sign to the disciples of the impending destruction of Jerusalem, so may this apostasy ["the decree enforcing the institution of the Papacy in violation of the law of God"—previous paragraph] be a sign to us that the limit of God's forbearance is reached. . . and that the angel of mercy is about to take her flight, never to return. The people of God. . . affliction and distress. . . trouble. . . The Judge of all the earth is soon to arise and vindicate His insulted authority. The mark of *deliverance* [Dan. 12:1] will be set upon the men who keep God's Commandments, who revere His law, and who refuse the mark of the beast. "

Notice the salient features: "The Roman armies" approach the city, Jerusalem. The Papal Sunday is to be enforced, probation will close, God's people will be in "trouble, " their "deliverance" is assured, for God arises to destroy His enemies. This is exactly what is taught in Dan. 11:45; 12:1.

The servant of the Lord has explicitly declared that "the written testimonies are *not* to give new light, but to impress vividly upon the heart the truths of inspiration already given. . . *Additional* truth is *not* brought out; but God has through the Testimonies simplified the great truths *already given*." 5T 665. Where in the Scriptures do we find the truth contained that as the approach of the literal armies upon literal Jerusalem was a sign of the impending destruction of the rejected Jerusalem, so the approach of "the beast" and "the false prophet" "and their armies" (see Rev. 19:19, 20) upon the spiritual city, Jerusalem, would be the sign that God is about to arise and destroy His enemies? We find all this in the correct interpretation of Dan. 11:45; 12:1.

In the Revelation, God's people are pictured as being "on Mount Sion" (Rev. 14:1). They are inside "the holy city"—compare Rev. 11:2 and 14:20. This is also taught in Joel 2:32: "The fugitives whom the Eternal calls shall be *inside* Jerusalem" (*Moffatt's Translation*). Joel 3; Ezek. 38,39; Zech. 14; etc., depict a gathering, or uniting, of the "nations," "heathen," or "gentiles" against spiritual Israel, and their destruction outside spiritual Jerusalem. The Spirit of Prophecy applies this gathering of the "heathen," or "nations," against Jerusalem as a picture of the enemies of the church making war upon her for her loyalty to God's Commandments. See EW 283, 284, 289; IT 183, 184; GC 657. The armies of the beast and the false prophet gather against the Lord "in the person of His witnesses" (7T 182; see also Rev. 17:14; Matt. 25:40). The destruction of those who oppose the people of God—their "Armageddon" slaughter—occurs *"without* the city" (Rev. 14:20) *"in* the valley of Jehoshaphat," or "Judgment" (Joel 3).

OUR LORD DEMONSTRATES THE TRANSITION FROM THE LITERAL TO THE SPIRITUAL.

Without a break in His second advent sermon, Jesus passed from literal to spiritual Rome, from literal Rome's destruction of the literal Jewish nation, city and temple (Matt. 24:15-20), to spiritual Rome's destruction of spiritual Israel—the spiritual city and temple of God (Matt. 24:21, 22). This "double" "spiritual" application of literal Rome's "war" on Israel is definitely presented in the Revelation. In Luke 21:24 we read the Master's prophecy: "Jerusalem shall be *trodden down* of the Gentiles." The Roman nation came, and Jerusalem was, and ever since has been, "trodden down" by "Gentiles." That was the "first" fulfillment of the Lord's prophecy (which was based upon the prophecies of Daniel, Matt. 24:15); the "double," "spiritual," application is presented by the Lord in Rev. 11:2: "But the court which is without the temple leave out, and measure it not; for it is given *unto the Gentiles:* and the holy city shall they [the Gentiles, as stated in Luke 21:24] *tread under foot* forty and two months."

The Papacy—the spiritual Romans—by persecuting the true church trod under foot the spiritual "holy city" as, similarly, the literal Romans brought destruction to literal Jerusalem in A.D. 70. This interpretation is given in GC 266: "Said the angel of the Lord: 'The Holy city (*the true church*) shall they tread under foot forty and two months. . .'

The King of the North at Jerusalem

"The periods here mentioned—'forty and two months,' and 'a thousand two hundred and threescore days'—are the same, alike representing the time in which *the church of Christ* was to suffer oppression *from Rome. . . The persecution of the church.*"

Thus the Lord has shown clearly the principle to be employed when interpreting the prophecies of Daniel concerning Jerusalem and the holy mountain. The literal Romans destroyed the literal city Jerusalem. In the Dark Ages, the spiritual Romans attacked "the holy city," the church, and trod it under foot. In the last days, it will again seek to trample it under foot, "and utterly to make away many" (Dan. 11:44), but in its attempt "he shall come to his end, and none shall help him" (Dan. 11:45).

The gathering of the nations to fight against Jerusalem, prophesied in Zech. 14:1-3, 12-14, had a local, partial fulfillment in A.D. 70 when the Roman armies (made up of many nationalities) were permitted to destroy the Jews' city because of their sins. God promised Israel: "Jerusalem shall be safely inhabited. And this shall be the *plague* wherewith the Lord will smite all the people that have *fought against Jerusalem*" (vs. 11, 12). The literal Romans were not plagued in "their *tongue*" (v. 12), for the Jews were not then God's people, but the Revelator, quoting from this passage when describing the people of spiritual Rome being smitten with the 5th plague, says: "And they gnawed their t*ongues* for pain" (Rev. 16:10). In GC 657; EW 289, God's servant quotes from Zech. 14:12, 13 when describing the fate of "those who have professed to be the *spiritual guardians of the people*" (GC 656), but have "*fought against Jerusalem*"—the true church. Thus the Spirit of Prophecy applies these *prophecies of attacks upon Jerusalem* in connection with the final conflict over the Sabbath.

In His second advent sermon, Jesus said: "When ye therefore shall see the abomination of desolation, spoken of by Daniel the prophet, stand in the *holy place* ["the glorious holy mountain"] (whoso readeth, let him understand)." Matt. 24:15. In Dan. 9:26, 27 we read of the coming of the Romans who would "destroy the city and the sanctuary; and the end thereof shall be with a *flood,* and unto the end of the war *desolations* are determined. . . and for the overspreading of abominations he shall make it desolate, even unto the consummation, and that determined shall be poured upon *the desolator.*" (See margin.) The enemy would "come in *like a flood*" but "the Spirit of the Lord," because of their sins, would "lift up a standard against him" (Isa. 59:19). The "abominations" (mentioned in Dan. 9:27; 11:31; 12:11) is the word employed in Scripture when referring to idolatrous worship. Commenting on Matt. 24:15, God's servant says: "When the *idolatrous standards* of the Romans should be set up in the holy ground, which extended some furlongs outside the city walls, then the followers of Christ were to find safety in flight" (GC 26).

In describing the spiritual Roman power, the Revelator designates her "the mother of harlots and *abominations* of the earth" (Rev. 17:5). Thus, in Rev. 17:4, 5 and also Matt. 24:15, Jesus applies, in a "double," "spiritual," sense, Daniel's prophecy concerning "the *abomination* of desolation." Both literal and spiritual Rome are designated by the same word: pagan Rome was an idolatrous power, and papal Rome, also, is an idolatrous power.

To His disciples, Jesus declared: "And when ye see Jerusalem compassed with armies, then know that the desolation thereof is nigh" (Luke 21:20). When that occurred they were to know that "the days of vengeance" had come (v. 22). As recorded in Matt. 24:15, 16, Jesus said: "When ye therefore shall see the abomination of desolation. . . stand in the holy place [Mark 13:14 "standing where it ought not"], (whoso readeth, let him understand:) then let them which be in Judea flee into the mountains. " As the sign for the flight of the disciples was that literal Rome was standing threateningly around Jerusalem, "*the holy place*," where she should not have stood, so, by the principle of the "double," "spiritual," application, the sign for the flight of God's people in the last days will be when spiritual Rome also stands "in the holy place"— "standing where it ought not"—presumptuously stands in the place of God by enforcing the keeping of Sunday in defiance of the Command of God.

It is acknowledged by all that the Papal assault on the church in the Dark Ages is described in Dan. 11:32-35. It is also acknowledged that this assault is described in Rev. 11:2 as an attack upon "*the holy city.*" Therefore the application that Dan. 11:45 refers to the gathering of the forces of spiritual Rome against the spiritual city of God, "in the glorious *holy* mountain," the church, is in harmony with what has already been made clear in the same prophecy.

Paul quotes from Dan. 11:36-39 when describing the rise and work of the Papacy: "That man of sin. . . as God *sitteth in the temple of God,* showing himself that he is God" (2 Thess. 2:3, 4). The Papacy is thus pictured as sitting "*in* the temple," God's church, which is represented as being "on the mount Sion," "in the glorious holy mountain." Thus by combining the prophetic delineations the Papacy is represented as being "in" Jerusalem during the Dark Ages. The events associated with the Reformation and the great Second Advent Movement have caused the Papacy to be more or less ejected from Jerusalem. But the prophetic word declares that the forces of evil will redouble their efforts to replace the Papacy fully within the church—that once more "the man of sin" will seek to show that "he is God" by demanding the world to obey his law instead of the Law of God. Thus Dan. 11:45 points to the last conflict in which "the man of sin, " "the beast, " "the little horn," will again encircle *"the holy city"* to subdue or to destroy the people of God. Thus the Spirit of Prophecy is in harmony with the Bible, when applying the Saviour's prophecy of Jerusalem being surrounded by Roman armies to the enforcement of Sunday laws.

CHAPTER TWENTY-TWO

WILL THE PAPACY REMOVE ITS SEAT OF POWER TO THE LITERAL CITY OF JERUSALEM?

Do the prophecies of Isa. 2:1-5 and Micah 4:1-4 teach that the Papacy will establish its seat of power in the literal city of Jerusalem? And will all nations receive the word of the Papacy as if it were the word of the Lord coming from that ancient historic city?

Such an interpretation is based upon a total misunderstanding of the prophecies of Isaiah and Micah. These contemporaneous prophets (compare Isa. 1:1 and Micah 1:1, and notice marginal dates. See also PK 322, 323, 330) were both burdened over the apostasy of God's people: they wrote concerning the judgments which would surely follow their departure from God and, as was the custom of the prophets, they also painted glowing pictures of the blessings which would follow obedience. The prophecies of Isa. 2:1-4 and Micah 4:1-4 contain the Lord's assurance of victory for His people and the certainty of the triumph of the work of the Saviour.

As is usual with all these precious promises for the church, the devil hides their grandeur by causing men to mis-apply them in connection with something to occur literally in Palestine. The belief of a Palestinian, military " Armageddon" is responsible for causing many, even among God's people, to misinterpret some of the most enlightening prophecies dealing with the conflict between truth and error. Many are not entirely free from error concerning God's rejection of the Jewish nation, because they do not fully appreciate the New Testament principle that the church, now "the Israel of God," inherits all the promises made anciently to God's people.

The prophecies of Isa. 2:1-4 and Micah 4:1-4 *concern the kingdom of the Messiah,* and not that of Satan's kingdom! In the book *Counsels to Parents, Teachers and Students,* p. 455, in the chapter entitled "The Word and Works of God," the Spirit of Prophecy quotes and applies Micah 4:2 (the parallel verse to Isa. 2:2) *not* to the work and words of Satan (!), but in connection with *the actual words of God Himself!* "What a God is our God! He rules over His kingdom with diligence and care" (CT 454). The Lord is *now* reigning "in mount Zion" (Micah 4:7) over His church. The Word of God is *now* going forth from His church, and it will continue to go from the church, and it will also go forth from the New Jerusalem throughout eternity, "when the Lord of hosts shall reign in mount Zion, and in Jerusalem, and before His ancients gloriously" (Isa. 24:23, and see also Isa. 60:11-20; 65:18, 19; 66:22, 23.

The Spirit of Prophecy makes the following comment on the prophecy found in Micah 4:11 concerning the gathering of "*many nations*" against "*Zion*" (mentioned in verses 2 and 7): "God will not fail *His church* in the hour of her greatest peril" (PK 538). The chapter heading of Isaiah 2 reads: "Isaiah prophesieth *the coming of Christ's kingdom*." The chapter heading of Micah 4 reads: "T*he glory and victory of the church*." Any other interpretation is entirely out of harmony with the Scriptures and the Spirit of Prophecy.

The declaration that the people shall turn their war weapons into agriculture implements describes the effect of God's Word. Through the Gospel people cease being warlike and learn to trust God to fight their battles for them. "Nation shall not lift up sword against nation, neither shall they learn war any more. BUT they shall sit every man under his vine and under his fig tree ; and *none shall make them afraid:* for the mouth of the Lord hath spoken it." When describing the work of "the BRANCH" (Luke 1:78, margin), the Saviour, Zechariah records the words of the Lord: "I will *remove the iniquity* of that land in one day. In that day, saith the Lord of hosts, shall ye call *every man his neighbour under the vine and under the fig tree*" (Zech. 3:10). The expression denotes security, trust, and confidence, and fitly describes the work of the Gospel. See also 1 Kings 4:25.

By comparing Isa. 2:3; Micah 4:2 with such passages as Jer. 3:17; 23:6; 31:6; 32:37; Zech. 8:22, it will be readily seen that the prophecies of Isa. 2:1-4 and Micah 4:1-4 *refer to the work of the Lord.* To apply them in relation to Satan's kingdom is a lamentable mis-interpretation.

The prophecies of Isaiah and Micah concerned "Jerusalem" "and many nations" (Isa. 2:1-3; Micah 1:1; 4:1-3). The prophet Zechariah also prophesied concerning "Jerusalem" "*and many nations.*" He said: "Jerusalem shall be inhabited as towns without walls [see Ezek. 38:8, 11] for the multitude of men and cattle therein: For I, saith the Lord, will be unto her a '*wall of fire round about,* and will be a glory in the midst of her. . . And *many nations* shall be *joined to the Lord* in that day" (Zech. 2:4, 5, 11). The Spirit of Prophecy applies this prophecy in connection with God's care over

His church and the work of making known the Gospel unto the world. See TM 16-18, and PK 581.

These prophecies (Isa. 2 and Micah 4) are sometimes employed to support the speculation that Satan will be crowned as Christ at Jerusalem. The Spirit of Prophecy does teach that "Satan himself will personate Christ." But there is no support either from Scripture or the Spirit of Prophecy for the belief that Satan will be crowned as Christ at Jerusalem. The servant of the Lord says: "*in different parts of the earth* Satan will manifest himself among men as a majestic being of dazzling brightness, resembling the description of the Son of God given by John in the Revelation" (GC 623, 624). For further references to Satan's impersonation of Christ, see also 5T 698; 8T 28; FE 471, 472; TM 411; 9T 16; EW 56. In all these references to this important feature of the future, *not once* is there a suggestion that the nations will be led by Satan to gather at Jerusalem, or Megiddo, to the coronation of Satan as Christ. The only fact which is sustained by revelation from God is that "*in different parts of the earth* Satan will manifest himself." Anything beyond this inspired statement is mere speculation based upon a misunderstanding of the prophecies of Isa. 2; Micah 4, and those concerning "Armageddon."

CHAPTER TWENTY-THREE

PROPHECY POINTS TO EUROPE—NOT PALESTINE—AS THE STORM CENTRE

Modern Babylon, mentioned in the book of Revelation (Rev. 17:5; 18:2, 7-9, etc.), *is centred in Europe,* and because that religio-political power is yet to wield a tremendous power over Europe and the whole of Christendom, *Europe comes into the purview of the prophecies,* wherein is depicted the last struggle in the great conflict between truth and error. See Rev. 17:12-14; etc.

The prophecy of Daniel, Chapter Two, commences with Nebuchadnezzar, the head of gold, in literal Babylon on the river Euphrates; it ends with the head of spiritual Babylon lifted to a place of prominence and power on the waters of the spiritual Euphrates. The head of Nebuchadnezzar's image was in literal Babylon on the river Euphrates; the *feet of the image rest upon Europe.* There is *no indication in any prophecy that the Papacy* will remove her seat from Europe: she is pictured as being *in Europe* until she comes to her well-merited end, with none to help.

In the prophecy of Daniel, chapter two, the Rock representing Christ, descending from the Government of God, *strikes the feet of the image* in the great slaughter of "Armageddon," when God strikes at His enemies, and destroys those who are destroying the earth (Rev. 11:18). Thus, in the first prophecy of Daniel, our attention is not directed to Palestine as the central place of the opposers of true religion in the final conflict between truth and error, but to EUROPE, for it is THERE that *the image is pictured as standing when Christ comes* to destroy His enemies. The fifth plague is definitely poured upon the throne of the beast—in EUROPE (see Rev. 16:10).

The prophecy of Dan. 11:45 does not refer to the Papacy removing the seat of its power to literal Jerusalem, but it does refer to the final assault by Papal powers against the true church of Jesus Christ. In making *"war"* against the remnant church (Rev. 12:17), the powers comprising modern Babylon make *"war"* against their Maker, Who reigns "in Zion." See 7T 141, 182;

TM 465 ; GC 623, 656; etc. The destruction of Satan's Babylonian forces in the great "Armageddon" slaughter will be *"without the city"* (Rev. 14:20; Joel 2:32 and Joel 3; Zech. 14; etc.), *"in* the valley of Jehoshaphat"—the world-wide "Valley of God's Judgment." *"Inside Jerusalem"* "shall be *deliverance,* as the Lord hath said, and in the *remnant* whom the Lord shall call" (Joel 2:32).

CHAPTER TWENTY-FOUR

WHEN WILL THE KING OF THE NORTH PLANT HIS TABERNACLES AT JERUSALEM?

*A*t *that time* shall Michael stand up. . . and *at that time* thy people shall be delivered" (Dan. 12:1). When Michael stands up, or commences His reign, probation closes for the human family; the deliverance of God's people occurs sometime later at the time of the 6th plague. Thus there are two events to occur at which time Michael will do something for His people. Twice occurs the expression "at that time," and in connection with it the words "thy people" are mentioned twice: hence the two actions of Michael are done on behalf of His people. Each time the expression "at that time" is used it refers to some action taken by Christ in opposing the work of the king of the north. *"At that time"* when "the king of the north," by the enforcement of Sunday laws, *is preparing to surround and to make "war"* on "the holy city," the church, "Michael shall stand up, the great Prince which standeth for the children of thy people;" *"at that time"* when "the king of the north" *causes the decree of death* to be passed upon Sabbath keepers for their continued loyalty to God's law, "thy people shall be delivered, everyone that shall be found written in the book" (Dan. 11:45; 12:1).

"There are: two events, brought to view in connection with the activities of the king of the north: (1) the king of the north plants the tabernacles of his palace at Jerusalem in readiness for the destruction of Jerusalem, and (2) his furious onslaught upon "the holy city" which ends in his total destruction. There are two events brought to view in connection with the activities of Michael on behalf of God's "people:" (1) He stands up, or "commences His reign, in order to, take kingly command to deal with the adversaries of His "people," (2) He delivers His "people" and destroys their adversaries. The king of the north comes to his end through the standing up of Michael—these are not unrelated events, as the "military interpretation" in relation to Turkey presents them. It is because His church is placed in a position of dire peril through the increasing power and fury of the king of the north that Michael stands up. As we have shown in another

87

place, the Lord Jesus, as the Lord and Deliverer of His people, took an oath that the activities of the king of the north would be brought to an end (see Dan. 12:6, 7, 11, 12). This oath is brought to view in the Revelator's description of events to transpire under the seventh Trumpet—compare Rev. 10:6, 7 and 11:15-19. The close of Christ's heavenly mediation means that no more mercy will be extended to the enemies of His church; then will commence the day of vengeance: "For it is *the day of the Lord's vengeance,* and the year of recompenses for *the controversy of Zion*" (Isa. 34:8), "and he put on the garments of vengeance. . . According to their deeds, accordingly He will repay, fury to His adversaries, recompense to His enemies" (Isa. 59:17, 18).

When Christ commences His reign (following the sounding of the seventh trumpet), it brings great rejoicing to His persecuted people: "We give thee thanks, O Lord God Almighty. . . because Thou hast to Thee taken Thy great power, and hast reigned" (Rev. 11:17). The seven plagues are definitely termed *"her [Babylon's] plagues"* (Rev. 18:4, 8). Instead of the king of the north being humbled by the plagues the Lord pours upon him, he becomes infuriated, and in his deception, blames the saints for his troubles, and is led to believe that by slaying them his troubles would end. God's servant says:

"It will be declared that men are offending God by the violation of the Sunday sabbath; that this sin has brought *calamities which will not cease until Sunday observance shall be strictly enforced;* and that those who present the claims of the fourth commandment, thus destroying reverence for Sunday, are troublers of the people, preventing their restoration to divine favour and temporal prosperity.

"Those who honour the law of God have been accused of bringing judgments upon the world, and *they will be regarded as the cause of the fearful convulsions of nature and the strife and bloodshed among men that are filling the earth with woe. . .*" (GC 587, 590, 614, 615).

"I saw the sword, famine, pestilence, and great confusion in the land. The wicked thought that we had brought the judgments upon them, and they rose up and took counsel to rid the earth of us, thinking that then the evil would be stayed" (EW 33, 34).

Thus will the king of the north lead his forces to destroy "the holy city." "And it shall come to pass at the same time when Gog [who comes from "the *north* parts," see Ezek. 39:1, 2] shall come against the land of Israel, saith the Lord God, that My fury shall come up in My face. For in My jealousy and in the fire of My wrath have I spoken. . ." (Ezek. 38:18-23).

CHRONOLOGICAL SEQUENCE

It is a custom of Bible prophets to bring the mind of the reader *down to the climax* and then to retrace his steps in order to present fuller details. In His second advent sermon, three times Jesus covers the course of history down to the end—see Matt. 24:1-14; then v. 15 to 28; then 29 to 51. In John's description of events under the seventh trumpet he gives a series of events to occur at that time (see Rev. 11:15-18), but in v. 19 he goes back to the opening of the heavenly temple in 1844 (see GC 433). The events he has enumerated under the seventh trumpet are definitely related to the Judgment. The ministry of our Lord in the heavenly temple from the time of 1844, commenced the winding up of earthly things. Thus the Revelator pointed to the climax of all things and then went back to show how all things depend upon the ministry of Christ in the heavenly temple. Space alone forbids us pointing out how this principle runs throughout the Bible.

In the study of the prophecies it is advisable to heed the sequence of events, but there will be seen a looping back in *connection with the climax.* We see this principle brought to view in Daniel's last prophecy, as well as in others that have preceded it. In Dan. 11:14 Rome is introduced into this prophecy, and immediately the angel points to the climax, saying: "B*ut they shall fall.*" Having clearly established Rome as the king of the north, and having brought into his description of that power the career of the first three of the Roman Emperors (vs. 17-21), the prophecy proceeds (v. 23) to outline some earlier history of that great empire which dominated the world at the time when Jesus of Nazareth—"the Prince of the Covenant" (v. 22)—took up His abode among men.

Bible students do not think it strange for the prophet, as he proceeds with his advance sketch of history, to break the chronological sequence or continuity of his narrative, and to step back into the past in order to record other interesting facts connected with the rise of the Roman power. This he does for the purpose of providing additional points of identification. Numerous instances of this practice will occur to the minds of all who are acquainted with sacred or secular literature.

Dan. 11:22 traces the work of Rome in destroying the Jewish nation, coming in on them like a "*flood*" (compare with Dan. 9:26), but this section of the prophecy closes with a reference to the work of Rome in *breaking* also "the Prince of the Covenant"—thus going back from A.D. 70 to A.D. 31. These two events are definitely connected in a climactic sense—the Jewish nation being permitted by

God to be destroyed because of their rejection of the Saviour.

Dan. 11:40-45 presents the scenes of the wounding of the king of the north, the healing of his wound, and of his subsequent successful activities as he leads the world in opposition to the people of God; in v. 45 the prophet proceeds to the climax—the end of this persecuting power. Then in Dan. 12:1 he connects up the activities of the king of the north in his attacks upon "the holy city"—*first,* his threatening attitude, then, *secondly,* his fury aroused to *slay the saints*—with what the Lord will do on behalf of His people in succouring their cause against the king of the north—*first,* His commencing to reign and to exercise His Almighty power to plague their enemies, and then, *secondly,* His intervention to *destroy their adversaries*: hence the two sets of events in the prophecy Dan. 11:45; 12:1. "*At that time*" [when the king of the north masses his forces threateningly around Jerusalem] "shall Michael stand up;" "*At that time*" [when the king of the north passes the death decree to slay the saints—to *destroy* "the holy city"] Michael delivers His people and destroys the king of the north: "he shall come to his end, and none shall help him."

We have come to the climax. Now, in our next chapter, we present details of events leading to that climax, thus further illustrating the principle we have followed in this chapter.

CHAPTER TWENTY-FIVE

THE KING OF THE NORTH IS ALREADY MARSHALING HIS FORCES TO SURROUND JERUSALEM

A s the church has taken the place of national Israel, she is presented in the prophecies *as if she were in Jerusalem.* When describing "the final conflict," the prophets describe the concerted action of Satan's kingdom against the remnant church as a gathering of mighty armies to attack "the holy city." It is this *symbolical* presentation of the final conflict which is so erroneously mis-applied literally in relation to a supposed military gathering of nations in Palestine. God's servant (who always presents the spiritual application of the prophecies which have a Palestinian setting), employing language taken from the prophecies of Joel 3; Ezek. 38; 39; Dan. 12:1, speaks of the final conflict, saying: "Satan wished to have the privilege of destroying the saints of the Most High; but Jesus bade His angels watch over them. God would be honoured by making a covenant with those who had kept His law, in the sight of the *heathen round about* [see Joel 3]. . . . Soon I saw the saints suffering great mental anguish. They seemed *to be surrounded* by the wicked inhabitants of the earth. . . God would not suffer His name to be reproached among the heathen [see Ezek. 39:7, etc.]. The time had nearly come when He was to manifest His mighty power, and gloriously *deliver* [see Dan. 12:1 and read on in EW] His saints." Under the chapter "Deliverance of God's people," God's servant says: "It was at midnight that God chose to *deliver* His saints. As the wicked were mocking *around them.* . . the saints beheld with solemn joy the tokens of their *deliverance*" (EW 282-285).

In these pages, God's servant couples together, in connection with the assault upon the people of God for their loyalty to God's Law, the prophecies of Joel 3; Ezek. 38; 39; Dan. 12:1, in which is de-picted a combined gathering of armies of evil bent upon the destruction of God's people within Jerusalem. Using the language of these prophecies, the Lord's servant describes the remnant church as being *"surrounded* by the wicked inhabitants of the earth," "the heathen *round about,"* "the wicked mocking *around them."* This, of course, is the Scriptural presentation. We shall now proceed to show that the gathering of the forces of the king of the north is now in progress: the king of the north is already marshaling his forces to march against "the holy city."

In the great *"war"* against the remnant (Rev. 12:17), the Papacy will eventually become supreme in the world. The Revelator, pointing to the closing scenes declares: *"All the world* wondered after the beast" (Rev. 13:3); *"all* that dwell upon the earth shall worship Him" (v. 8). "These [the nations of Christendom] have one mind, and shall give their power and strength unto the beast. These shall make *war* with the Lamb [Who, in Rev. 14:1, is pictured as being with His church upon Mt. Zion], and the Lamb shall overcome them. . . and they that are with Him [on Mt. Zion] are called, and chosen, and faithful" (Rev. 17:12-14). Under the figure of a woman, the apostate church will say: "I am a queen, and am no widow, and shall see no sorrow. Therefore shall her plagues come in one day. . . for strong is the Lord God Who judgeth her" (Rev. 18:7, 8).

The king of the north, who is also called the beast in the Revelation, leads Satan's forces *against the Lamb and His church upon Mt. Zion:* The Revelator describes this spiritual conflict in realistic imagery: "And I saw the beast, and the kings of the earth, and their armies, *gathered together* to make war against Him that sat on the horse, and against His army" (Rev. 19:19, 20). He pictures Satan, with his hosts of evil spirits, working through the dragon (the State), the beast, and the false prophet *to gather* "the kings of the earth and of the whole world. . . to the battle of that great day of God Almighty. . . . And he gathered them together to a place called in the Hebrew tongue Armageddon" (Rev. 16:13-16). This "war" against the remnant church (Rev. 12:17; Dan. 11:44) will be waged with the greatest ferocity and power. "The coming struggle will be marked with a terrible intensity *such as the world has never witnessed"* (GC xi). The forces of Babylon will plan to wipe out completely all those who will remain loyal to the Law of God. The spirit of hatred and intensity will increase as the Spirit of God is withdrawn from the earth. Thus the whole world will "gather" against the Lord and His church on Mt. Zion. That gathering is now taking place and, at the time of the 6th plague, this gathering will be complete. This is the teaching of the Bible and of the Spirit of Prophecy.

When God's people heed the call: "Come out of her [Babylon], My people" (Rev. 18:4), they *"gather together. . .* from the four corners of the earth" (Isa. 11:11, 12). Commenting upon these verses in Isaiah which describe the *"gathering"* of spiritual Israel, God's servant, in the chapter "The Gathering Time," says: "In the *gathering* time God will heal and bind up His people. . . in the *gathering*, when God has set His hand to gather His people" (EW 74). On page 75, 76 the Lord's servant strongly condemns those who look to Palestine for the fulfillment of such promises to Israel. The *"gathering"* of Israel in preparation for the day of the Lord, referred to by the Lord's servant in EW 74-76, is explained on p. 86 to refer to the *"union"* of God's people, "and to the fact that He had begun to *unite* and to raise up His people." Here, as in other places throughout her writings, God's servant declares that the meaning of the word *"gather"* (mentioned in so many of the last-day prophecies—see Isa. 54:15; 60:4; Ezek. 38:8; 39:27, 28; Joel 3:2, 11; Zech. 14:2, 3, 12; Rev. 16:14, 16; 19:19) is *"union," "unite."* In giving us the meaning of the Greek word "sun" (from whence is derived the word "gather" employed in Rev. 16:14, etc.) Dr. Strong says it denotes *"union"*—which is same word employed by God's servant in explaining the meaning of the expression *"gather together"* in the prophecy of Isa. 11:11, 12. It is by this spiritual *"union"* that believers in the Lord are being *"builded together* for an habitation of God through the Spirit" (Eph. 2:21, 22).

Not only when referring to the spiritual "gathering together" of Israel does God's servant employ the word *"union"* or *"united,"* but also when describing the strengthening of the opposing forces. "The agencies of evil *are combining* their forces and *consolidating.* They *are strengthening* for the last great crisis" (9T 11). Commenting upon the "gathering" of the tares (see Matt. 13:30, 40), God's servant says: "Can we not see how earnestly Satan *is* at work *binding* the tares in bundles, *uniting* the elements of his kingdom, that he may gain control of the world? This work of binding up the tares *is going forward* far more rapidly than we imagine" (5T 383, 384). "They [men] *have united.* . . . They are represented in God's Word as being bound in bundles to be burned. Satan is *uniting* his forces for perdition" (6T 242).

In giving an inspired explanation of the "gathering" of the nations to "Armageddon," mentioned in Rev. 16:14, God's servant explicitly shows that the word "gather" refers to the spiritual "union" of the elements of Satan's kingdom: "The spirits of devils will go forth to the kings of the earth and to the whole world [*obviously* the reference is to Rev. 16:13, 14], to fasten them in deception, and urge them on to *unite* with Satan in his last struggle against the government of Heaven" (GC 624). With such clear and definite statements from the Spirit of Prophecy there should be no question as to the meaning of the gathering to Armageddon.

"Every soul that is not fully surrendered to God. . . will form an alliance ["unite" or "gather"] *with Satan* against heaven, and join in battle against the Ruler of the universe" (TM 465). By comparing this statement with *Weymouth's Translation* of Rev. 16:14, we readily see that God's servant is again interpreting the meaning of the "gathering" to Armageddon—a *uniting* of the forces of good and evil "against the government of Heaven," and *not* a gathering of nations literally to Palestine. God's servant often refers to the "uniting" of the forces of evil when describing the final conflict over the Sabbath—see 5T 449; GC 582, 604, 605, 607, etc. The true interpretation of the prophetic imagery of the Apocalypse reveals that this teaching is exactly what is portrayed in the Revelator's graphic depiction of the final conflict.

God's people are urged to study "to understand the progress of events in the *marshaling of the nations for the final conflict of the great controversy*" (8T 307). God's people should know that "already the inhabitants of the earth *are marshaling* under the leading of the prince of darkness. . . . The Law of God is made void" (8T 49).

In *The Great Controversy*, pp. 561, 562, we are given the correct interpretation of the work of evil spirits in "gathering" "the kings of the earth and of the whole world. . . to the battle of that great day of God Almighty:"

"Satan *has long been preparing* for his final effort to *deceive the world.* . . . He has not yet reached the full accomplishment of his designs; but it [Satan deceiving the world to join him in his rebellion against God's Law] will be reached in the last remnant of time. Says the prophet: 'I saw three unclean spirits like frogs; . . . they are the spirits of devils, working miracles, which go forth unto the kings of the earth and of *the whole world,* to gather them to the battle of that great day of God Almighty' (Rev. 16:13,14). Except those who are kept by the power of God, through faith in His Word, *the whole world* will be swept into the ranks of *this delusion.* The people are fast being lulled into a fatal security, to be awakened only by the outpouring of the wrath of God."

Thus we see that the Lord interprets the "gathering" of the nations to Armageddon as "the whole world" being *deceived* into *joining* the "ranks" of the forces of evil; they *"unite* with Satan in his last struggle against the government of Heaven." Satan has been *deceiving* mankind for a *"long"* time; he wants "to deceive *the world.* . . He has not *yet* reached the *full* accomplishment of his designs;

but it will be reached" by the time of the battle of Armageddon. As by the 6th plague "the whole world" is said to be "gathered" by miracle-working spirits who have deceived earth's multitudes, and that is "the *full* accomplishment of his designs," and as that work of deception is said to be the gathering or *uniting* of "the kings of the earth and of the whole world," the "gathering" must already be in progress; "*already* the inhabitants of the earth *are marshaling* under the leading of the prince of darkness." The "gathering" pictured in Rev. 16:14 does not refer to some sudden military manoeuvre by nations to Megiddo, but refers to the *culmination* of the work of deception carried on through the years by Satan as he prepares to "*unite*" the world to "*join*" him "in his last struggle" against God. By the time of the sixth plague "the wicked have *fully united* with Satan in his *warfare against God*" (GC 656).

The spirits of evil are "*already. . . marshaling*" the nations to fight "against the government of Heaven"—soon those who make "*war*" against their Maker and His church will come to their end, and none shall help them. "Already" in progress is the gathering of God's people to be with Christ on Mt. Zion. Right in the midst of the picture of the gathering of the forces of evil against the Lord and His people, the Saviour proclaims a solemn warning to His people to watch and keep their garments—see Rev. 16:15. But the watching and the keeping of garments apply *now*—it will be too late after probation closes to get ready. It is *now* before probation closes and while the evil spirits are gathering the nations to make war against God and His people that God's people, too, are to make their preparations. They must now heed the call of Christ to stand "with Him" on Mt. Zion in the garments of righteousness which He provides, and to be "chosen" before mercy's door closes, and, by loyalty to His commands, be proved "faithful" (Rev. 14:1; 17:14). Thus when the gates of "the holy city" are shut for ever and no more sinners will be permitted to enter into it, the saved—"they that do His Commandments" (Rev. 22:14)—will be "*within* Jerusalem," whilst the unsaved will be outside "in the valley of God's Judgment" (Joel 2:32; ch. 3; Rev. 22:15; etc.).

During the Dark Ages, the king of the north, the man of sin, the son of perdition, not only planted the tabernacles of his palace "in the glorious holy mountain" (2 Thess. 2:3-5), but at that time he also trod "the holy city" under foot for 1260 years (see Rev. 11:1, 2). Through His loyal servants in the work of the Reformation, the Lord caused the king of the north to receive "a deadly wound" (Rev. 13:3), and thus he withdrew from God's "holy city." But the beast has revived; the power of the king of the north returns, and

Satan is waiting the day when he will again hurl all his forces against "the holy city," the church. In the Dark Ages "it was given unto him to make war with the saints, and to overcome them" (Rev. 13:7). As this "war" was said to be that of treading under foot "the holy city" (Rev. 11:2), so the "war" against the remnant (Rev. 12:17) in connection with the enforcement of Sunday laws is also likened to an attack upon "the holy city" (Dan. 11:44, 45). Then, the king of the north will *again* plant his tabernacle outside Jerusalem and prepare "to destroy" it "utterly." But this time the Lord will not permit the king of the north, the man of sin, to harm His church. Instead, His unmingled wrath will be poured out upon the assembled hosts who will be gathered "in the valley of Jehoshaphat" before His holy habitation: "The Lord shall roar *out of Zion,* and utter His voice *from Jerusalem;* and the heavens and the earth shall shake: but the Lord will be the hope of His people, and the strength of the children of Israel [those "*in* mount Zion and *in* Jerusalem" will be *delivered,* Joel 2:32]. So shall ye know that I am the Lord your God *dwelling in Zion, My holy mountain*: then shall *Jerusalem be holy,* and there shall no strangers pass through her any more" (Joel 3:16, 17).

The persecution of the church during the Dark Ages is declared to be a "*war*" (Rev. 13:7), also the *treading underfoot* of "*the holy city*" (Rev. 11:2), and also the *flooding of the river Euphrates* (Rev. 12:15, 16; Josh. 24:2, 4, 14, 15; Isa. 8:7, 8; etc.). Thus the final phase of the conflict between the forces of good and evil is again a "*war*" (Rev. 12:17), an *attack upon* "*the holy city*" (Dan. 11:45; Rev. 14:20; Joel 3; Zech. 14), *and the flooding of the river Euphrates* (Rev. 16:12). In "the *battle* of that great day *of God* Almighty" (Rev. 16:14), the Lord makes "*war*" (Rev. 19:11-20) upon the multitudes that are gathered against His "holy city" (Dan. 11:45; 12:1; Zech. 14:2, 3, 12, 13, Rev. 14:20): He dries up the flooding waters of the Euphrates (Rev. 16:12; Jer. 50:38; Isa. 44:27; etc.)—the river of Babylon (Rev. 17:1, 15; Jer. 51:13, etc.) which is declared to be "in the *north* country" (Jer. 46:6, 10). Thus *the ending of the king of the north and the drying up of the waters of the Euphrates refer to the same power*: the doom of the forces of Babylon.

CHAPTER TWENTY-SIX

DANIEL'S LAST PROPHECY OUTLINES THE GREAT CONTROVERSY BETWEEN CHRIST AND SATAN

When introducing this prophecy, Daniel said: "The thing was true, but the time appointed was *long" (Dan.* 10:1). The margin for "long" is *"great."* The original word employed here for "long" is not the same as that used in Dan. 8:13; 12:6. Dr. Strong defines it and its derivatives: "Great (in any sense). . . mighty. . . sore. . . to twist. . . be much set by." *Dr. Moffatt's Translation* reads: "The true revelation of *a great conflict."* The *Annotated Paragraph Bible* says: "Rather *'the warfare was great:'* see note on Job 7:1." Daniel's last prophecy, therefore, must be read in the light of the spiritual warfare that has ensued down the ages.

In Dan. 10:13, 20, Gabriel pulled back the curtain and revealed the part played by the angelic hosts in this fierce conflict. He said to Daniel: "And now I will return to fight with the prince of Persia." By verses 13, 20 we must not understand a literal fight, a literal battle. Throughout his three weeks' fasting and praying, Daniel may have felt the loneliness of struggling to forward the cause of Christ. Gabriel's message enabled him to see that the angels were cooperating with him in the great spiritual war being waged. The Lord's servant says: "The great controversy between good and evil will *increase in intensity to the very close of time"* (GC ix). It was to reveal light upon this mighty drama, this all-important subject, that Daniel's last prophecy, particularly, was given.

Both the books of Daniel and Revelation were given to reveal the fierce war between the forces of good and evil. Everything in them was given with this express purpose in mind. Nothing superfluous or extraneous is brought into the prophetic outlines. By applying Dan. 11:36-39 to the French Revolution, and vs. 40-45; 12:1 to Turkey and the supposed gathering of nations to Palestine for "Armageddon," the vital facts concerning the spiritual conflict are hidden by that which is entirely irrelevant to the express purpose for which they were given!

Louis F. Were

Daniel's last prophecy commences with Satan seeking to hinder
the work of God in rebuilding and restoring Jerusalem after the
Babylonian captivity; it also concludes with Satan seeking to destroy
the people of God (Dan. 11:44, 45; 12:1). Only by Michael, the great
Prince Who intercedes on Israel's behalf, is the work carried forward
at the commencement (note Dan. 10:2, 12, 13, 21), and only by His
Almighty power are the people of God delivered from Satan's effort
to destroy them in the final conflict (Dan. 11:44, 45; 12:1).

This last prophecy was given to Daniel after his three weeks'
fasting and praying (Dan. 10:2). Daniel was deeply distressed
because so few of his people returned to their land of promise, also
because the work of God was meeting with Satanic opposition.
Very shortly (about two years) after the expiration of the seventy
years' captivity and the decree of Cyrus authorizing the restoration
of Jerusalem, enemies of the returned exiles "weakened the hands
of the people of Judah, and troubled them in building," even in
sending "hired counsellors" to the court of Cyrus. These "hired
counsellors" worked "against them, to frustrate their purpose, all
the days of Cyrus" and later (Ezra 4:4, 5). The mighty Gabriel had
been sent to Cyrus (Dan. 10:13, 20) to influence him to go forward
with his work in behalf of restoring the temple at Jerusalem. But
there was a delay of twenty-one days because Satan endeavored to
influence Cyrus against complying with God's will. During this
time Daniel prayed for an understanding of his vision. Finally our
Lord Jesus, referred to here as "Michael," the first of the princes
(Dan. 10:13, margin), the Head of the angelic hosts, "the Archan-
gel" (Jude 9)—the angels are said to be "*His* angels," Rev. 12:7—
"came to help." Thus this prophecy commences with the difficul-
ties the people of God encountered from Satanic sources, difficul-
ties so great that our Lord Himself came to the rescue and took
personal charge of the situation. The prophecy also closes with the
greater distresses God's people will surely encounter in the closing
scenes, distresses so great that again the Lord will come to the
rescue and take personal charge of the situation—He will deliver
His people from imminent peril (Dan. 12:1).

Daniel was greatly distressed by the opposition God's people
met with as they returned to Jerusalem to rebuild God's temple
and city. The Lord gave Daniel this prophecy to describe the far
greater troubles awaiting the people of God down the centuries
(Dan. 10:14). The distresses that would come to the Jewish people
through the wars of the Seleucid and Ptolemaic empires would
lead to even greater dangers and perils for the people of God. The
Roman power would arise that would eventually break up the

Jewish nation (Dan. 11:15). But the greatest troubles would come to God's true people, not from so-called "heathen" sources, but from a power which, while making the high claim of being "the true church," would actually be led of Satan to inflict the most fearful sorrows upon God's people. This power, after the Dark Ages, through God's overruling Providence, would be held back for a time while the work of God would be completed, just as God's providences enabled Israel to complete the rebuilding of Jerusalem *"even in troublous times"* (Dan. 9:25; see also Ezra and Nehemiah). As the work of God progressed, the opposition to it became more and more bitter and determined. See Neh. 4:6-8; etc. Thus will it be in the closing up of the work of God.

More and more the power of God will be poured out to meet Satan's opposition. Finally, Satan will stir up the powers of evil—the king of the north and all of his forces—to subdue or destroy the people of God. But Christ will deliver His people in this final attempt to destroy them. This is a brief summary of Daniel's last prophecy: it is concerned wholly with this spiritual conflict. There are no "side-issues" or irrelevancies, such as Turkish history, brought into the prophecy.

Daniel's last prophecy is the enlargement of all his earlier prophecies. In His second advent sermon, Jesus enlarged upon the book of Daniel, and with special significance He refers to Daniel's last two prophecies concerning the Roman attack upon Jerusalem. In the Revelation, our Lord enlarges upon His second advent sermon. Thus we see the importance of Daniel's last prophecy (chapters 10 to 12), and also its relationship to the book of Revelation. Near the conclusion of Daniel's last prophecy we are informed of an attack made upon the people of God by the king of the north (Dan. 11:44; 12:1). In His second advent sermon, Jesus declares that just before His return the true followers of God will be smitten by professing Christians (Matt. 24:48-51). When describing earth's final scenes, the Revelator enlarges upon the fact that the final peril to the church will come from professing Christian bodies—the beast and the false prophet (Revelation, chapters 13 to 19). Thus the term "the king of the north" refers to these professing Christian powers whose opposition to the work and people of God looms so large in the Revelator's description of the final conflict between the forces of good and evil.

The importance of Daniel's last prophecy and its relationship to the book of Revelation will be recognized by noting that both commence with a "revelation of Jesus Christ" (compare Dan. 10:5, 6 and Rev. 1:13-17). In both, the glory of His person fills Daniel and John with awe and fear. In both, Jesus comforts His faithful servants with the knowledge that while He possesses Almighty power, His power is used to show Himself strong on behalf of those whose hearts are perfect towards Him. How fitting that both Daniel's last prophecy and the Revelation, which is the enlargement of that prophecy, should commence with a description of Jesus in His purity and power, and also in His capacity of the High Priest interceding on behalf of His people. If the display of His power filled His loyal subjects with fear, how will His adversaries fare when that Almighty power is used on behalf of His persecuted people!

The connection between Daniel's last prophecy and the book of Revelation is further seen upon examining the Epanados employed in the first chapter of Revelation. These eight Old Testament texts are employed in exalting Jesus as the Destroyer of Babylon and the Deliverer of His people. These eight texts are so arranged that the first text is quoted from the same Old Testament book as the eighth, the second Old Testament quotation is from the same book as the second to last; the third from the same book as the third from the last; the central ones—the fourth from the first and fourth from the last—are front the same Old Testament book. The following sets forth this Epanados, employed in Rev. 1 to declare Christ's Lordship:

    (1) Rev. 1:5. Isa. 55:4.
        (2) 7. Dan. 7:13.
            (3) 7. Zech. 12:10.
                (4) 8. Isa. 41:4; 44:6; 48:12.
                (4) 11. Isa. 41:4; 44:6; 48:12.
            (3) 12. Zech. 4:2.
        (2) 13-15. Dan. 7:9, 13, 22; 10:5, 6.
    (1) 16. Isa. 49:2.

The first quotation, like the eighth, is from the book of Isaiah. The first text from Isaiah says that the Messiah would be "a Leader and a Commander to the people." The eighth—the last—quotation in this Epanados, in bringing us back to Isaiah (49:2), shows how the Lord proves Himself to be the "Leader and Commander to the people": "Out of His mouth went a sharp two-edged sword" (Rev. 1:16; Isa. 49:2). The destruction of His enemies by the sword of His mouth, referred to in Isa. 49:2, is again repeated in Rev. 19:15, 21: "Out of His mouth goeth a sharp sword, that with it He should smite the nations." In Rev. 19:11-21 the Lord is pictured as coming to wage "war" on the beast—the king of the north—and the false prophet who have been making "war" upon His remnant people (Rev. 12:17).

In the comforting message given in Isaiah (ch. 40-48) concerning the overthrow of Babylon, and the deliverance of His people, Jesus, the Almighty Son of God, repeatedly referred to Himself as "the first and the last." See Isa. 41:4; 43:10; 44:6; 48:12. These are the verses Jesus quotes in the Revelation when referring to Himself as "the first and the last." In Isaiah, Jesus thus speaks of Himself when encouraging His people with the promise that He would overthrow their Babylonian enemies and bring them deliverance. In the Revelation He again repeatedly refers to Himself as "the first and the last" to encourage His church that He will overthrow spiritual Babylon and bring about their eternal deliverance (see Rev. 1:8, 11; 2:8; 21:6; 22:13).

Notice the connection between Isaiah's prophecy, the Revelation, and Daniel's last prophecy: they are each dealing with the overthrow of Babylon; they each draw attention to "the first and the last"; they each deal with the deliverance of God's people. In the prophecy of Isaiah, Cyrus is named as the one who would overthrow Babylon and liberate God's people. Daniel's last prophecy commences with Cyrus (Dan. 10:1) the destroyer of Babylon and the deliverer of God's people, it ends (Dan. 12:1) with Jesus the destroyer of modern Babylon and the Deliverer of God's people. Thus Daniel's last prophecy is connected up with Isaiah's graphic prophecy of the doom of Babylon in which Jesus is repeatedly said to be "the first and the last." Cyrus (the name means the "sun"), the *first* king in the prophecy, God's "anointed," or "messiah" (see Isa. 45:1), is a type of the *last* king in the prophecy—Jesus "the Sun of Righteousness," "the Shepherd King," God's "Anointed," or "Messiah"—who will come to overthrow spiritual Babylon by drying up her waters (Rev. 16:12, etc.), and will bring deliverance to His people.

At His second advent, the "Leader and Commander" (Isa. 55:4; Rev. 1:5) of the forces of righteousness will overthrow the forces of Babylon at "Armageddon." This final conflict is enlarged upon in Rev. 19:11-21. The "sharp sword" (Isa. 49:2) mentioned in the last of the eight quotations in the Epanados of Rev. 1 (v. 16), is seen in action (Rev. 19:15) in the slaughter of "Armageddon," which results in the complete destruction of spiritual Babylon.

The linen garments worn by our Lord, when seen by Daniel at the time he was given his last prophecy (Dan. 10:5, 6), would indicate His priestly work—particularly His High Priestly ministration on the day of Atonement (see Lev. 16:4). In this connection, notice that a part of the description given of our Lord in Rev. 1 comes from the description given of Him in Dan. 7 in connection with the Judgment: the Judgment would sit and the Papacy would be destroyed (see Dan. 7:11, 26). As in the commencement of Daniel's last prophecy the priestly work of Christ is indicated, so the end of that prophecy brings us to the time when He ceases His mediation in the heavenly temple (Dan. 12:1). The king of the north gathers his forces (Dan. 11:44, 45) against the people of God just as the Lord is about to close His heavenly ministry: "At that time shall Michael stand up, the great Prince [mentioned in the commencement of the prophecy, see Dan. 10:13] which standeth for the children of thy people" (Dan. 12:1).

That Daniel's last prophecy deals with the great controversy between Christ and Satan is also obvious from the fact that this prophecy commences and ends with Jesus being termed *"Michael, the first of the Princes"* (Dan. 10:13), Who comes to wage war against the machinations of Satan. When the Revelator describes how the '"war" began in heaven with Satan's machinations against His Father's Government, He says: " And there was *war* in heaven: *Michael* and His angels fought against the dragon" (Rev. 12:7). As Daniel's last prophecy describes the great conflict between Christ and Satan from Daniel's day until the king of the north comes to his end while he is gathered to destroy "the holy city," the people of God, so the Revelator also traces the conflict down through the ages from the time Michael opposed Satan in Heaven until the forces of Satan are destroyed as they surround '"the holy city," "the true church" (see GC 266; Rev. 11:2; 14:20).

CHAPTER TWENTY-SEVEN

WHY DANIEL'S LAST PROPHECY WAS GIVEN "BY THE SIDE OF THE GREAT RIVER" (DAN. 10:4)

There is a significant reason why Daniel had his last prophecy on the banks of "the great river" (Dan. 10:4). It was there that the Lord Jesus revealed Himself to the prophet (vs. 5-9); it was there that the whole of the prophecy found in chapters 10 to 12 was given to him. After outlining the course of events *leading to the final acts of the king of the north,* the river is again brought to view in the prophecy: "Then I Daniel looked, and, behold, there stood other two, the one on *this side of the bank of the river,* and the other on *that side of the bank of the river.* And one said to the Man clothed in linen [our Lord Jesus], *which was upon the waters of the river,* How long shall it be to the end of these wonders? And I heard the Man clothed in linen, which was upon the waters of the river, when He held up His right hand and His left hand unto heaven, and sware by Him that liveth for ever that it shall be for a time, times, and a half; and when *he [the king of the north is the antecedent of the pronoun "he"]* shall have accomplished to scatter the power of the holy people, and these things shall be finished" (Dan. 12:5-7). Thus we see that "the great river" is not only mentioned at the commencement of this prophecy but is also brought in toward its close, where, *for emphasis,* it is mentioned four times, *when dealing with the king of the north coming to his end.*

Notice the connection between the Lord standing upon the waters of "the great river" when taking the oath to comfort His church concerning the time limit of Papal supremacy (Dan. 12:5-7)—thus the conquests of the king of the north are all under Christ's supervision and control. The prophecy declares that the king of the north '"shall sweep through many lands *like an overwhelming flood"* (Dan. 11:40, *The American Translation*). Though the king of the north with all his hordes shall sweep through "many countries" and, entering "also into the glorious land" of Israel, will threaten to engulf Jerusalem with his gigantic tidal wave, the Lord will control that flood: in the final conflict, He will deliver His people from seemingly imminent death.

The picture of a mighty angel on either side of the river and with the Omnipotent Lord standing upon the rushing waters surely indicates that they are under Heavenly cognizance and control. Waters signify people (Rev. 17:15), and His standing upon the waters denotes *His dominion over all.* "The *Lord sitteth upon the flood;* yea, the Lord *sitteth King for ever"* (Ps. 29: 10).

The significance of the emphasis (four times repeated) in the ending of this prophecy of the Lord standing upon this river has a wonderful message of comfort for the people of God. This prophecy was given to outline the conflicts and perils of the church until the end of time. In the dark mysteries of God's providences, He permits His church to suffer at the hands of His enemies. But His hand is over their activities. He permits only that which will purify His people. Thus the significance of the statement: "Many shall be purified, and made white and tried" (Dan. 12:10) *given in answer to the questions concerning the length of time the king of the north would be permitted to continue his persecution of the church* (see vs. 6, 8). Often in their troubles God's people have cried *"How long* shall it be to the end of these wonders?"* (Dan. 12:6; 8:13; Ps. 74:10; Zech. 1:12; Rev. 6:10). In this prophecy, the Lord points to the time when all persecution shall cease; when the king of the north, the chief persecutor of His people, will come to his end by the intervention of the Lord of the church.

In the days of our Lord's earthly pilgrimage, the disciples had a trying experience on the sea of Galilee. Their little "ship" was "tossed with waves: for the winds were contrary" (Matt. 14:22-27). It was then that Jesus came to them "walking on the sea" and revealed Himself as the Master of the raging waters and the Helper of His troubled disciples (vs. 27-33). The oath Jesus took (Dan. 12:7) was to encourage His people (just as the oath God gave anciently was for "the heirs of promise" Heb. 6:13-20).

In Dan. 12:7 our Lord is said to take an oath with feet on the waters of the great river and both hands toward heaven. It is to this oath that the Revelator refers in Rev. 10:5-7. In both these prophecies, the Lord solemnly promises His church that they shall not much longer be obliged to suffer for His sake. The persecutors will be destroyed, and the saints will triumph eternally. The oath contains this solemn promise: "that there should be time no longer" or, as given in *Dr. Moffatt's Translation*: "There shall be no more delay" (Rev. 10:6). Though God has seemingly delayed His judgments upon the world, He promises that the time will come when there "shall be no more delay." No longer will He withhold His hand of vengeance against the persecutors of His people.

By comparing Rev. 10:5-7 with Rev. 11:15 we learn that the oath "there shall be no more delay" has reference to the time when the Lord ceases His mediatorial work and commences His reign as earth's rightful King. Rev. 10:7 reads: "But in the days of the voice of the seventh angel. . . the mystery of God should be finished." Rev. 11:15 R.V. reads: "And the seventh angel sounded. . . the kingdom of the world is become the kingdom of our Lord." Then, the sovereignty over the world will be our Lord's. Then, He shall show "Who is the blessed and only Potentate, the King of kings, and Lord of lords" (1 Tim. 6:15, see also Rev. 17:14; 19:16). When Michael stands up to avenge His people, then the king of the north comes to his end (Dan. 11:45; 12:1).

Anciently, the Lord "willing more abundantly to show unto the heirs of promise the immutability of His counsel, confirmed it by an oath" (Heb. 6:17). The oath given in Daniel's last prophecy and repeated in the Revelation is God's message of blessed assurance that He will not long delay His intervention on their behalf. And in Daniel's last prophecy the Lord reveals the events which will lead up to the final conflict: He warns His people of the final persecution at the hands of the king of the north, but His assurance is that He stands upon the waters of the great river, which typify the persecuting power of the king of the north—He controls the flood and when He so desires He will dry up the waters of Babylon's "great river" (Rev. 16:12). As Cyrus, who is mentioned at the commencement of this prophecy (Dan. 10:1), dried up the waters of the Euphrates as part of his strategy in the overthrow of Babylon, so Jesus will also dry up the waters of the great river Euphrates as part of His plan for the over-throw of spiritual Babylon.

CHAPTER TWENTY-EIGHT

THE KING OF THE NORTH COMES TO HIS END:
THE WATERS OF THE EUPHRATES ARE DRIED UP.

T he river Euphrates is termed "great" five times in the Bible (see Gen. 15:18; Deut. 1:7; Josh. 1:4; Rev. 9:14; 16:12). The Hiddekel, or Tigris, is never thus designated in the Scriptures. The *Pocket Commentary* says: "Hiddekel, the river Tigris, *a branch of the Euphrates*." In his comments on Dan. 10:4, Uriah Smith says: "By the river Hiddekel the Syriac understands the Euphrates; the Vulgate, Greek, and Arabic, the Tigris ; hence Wintle concludes that the prophet had this vision at the place where these rivers unite, as they do not far from the Persian Gulf."—*Thoughts on Daniel and Revelation,* p. 220.

The connection between the region of the river Euphrates and the king of the north is apparent when observing that the Scriptures speak of "the *north* country *by the river Euphrates*" (Jer. 46:2, 6, 10). The Babylonians came from the north (Jer. 1:13-15; 4:6; 6:1; 25:9, 26; 46:20, 24) they flooded the land of Israel like the overflowing of the waters of the Euphrates (Isa. 8:7-8; see also Isa. 28:2; Jer. 47:2, etc.)

The river Euphrates is employed in Scripture as the symbol to represent *invading, destroying forces.* This is how it is employed in both Rev. 9 and 16. In Rev. 9 the Euphrates is employed to *represent invading, destroying forces*—the Ottoman Empire that *invaded and destroyed the remnants of the Roman Empire*. In the prophecy, the emphasis is upon the work of destruction wrought by the Ottoman empire. Observe carefully Rev. 9:5, 10, 11, margin, 15, 18.

The Euphrates in Rev. 16:12 is employed to symbolize *invading, destroying forces*—the persecuting power of spiritual Babylon. In Josh. 24:2, 3, 14, 15, the Euphrates is termed "the flood." In Rev. 12:15, 16 "the flood" (that is, the Euphrates) refers to the persecution of the church during the Dark Ages. As that persecution is also called a "war" (Rev. 13:7; Dan. 7:21), we know that the Revelator's statement that the dragon will make "war" on the remnant (Rev. 12:17) means that the Euphratean flood of persecution in the Dark Ages is to be repeated in the final conflict, and the drying up of the

Euphrates has reference to the cessation of the Babylonian persecution of the church by the intervention of God. "Babylon," "the great
whore," is definitely described as one "that sitteth *upon many
waters*" (Rev. 17:1). As the margin indicates, this is a quotation from
Jer. 51:13, which refers to literal Babylon "that dwellest *upon many
waters*." Babylon was built upon the Euphrates. As the Revelator
had already made use of the "flood" when referring to the persecution at the hands of spiritual Babylonians in the Dark Ages (Rev.
12:15, 16) and as, in Rev. 17, he has described spiritual Babylon as
being built upon the Euphrates, his mention of the Euphrates in
Rev. 16:12 could have reference only to the drying up of the
Babylonian waters of persecution by God's intervention.

The invasion of the land of Israel and the attack upon the
people of God are likened to the flooding of the land of Israel by
the waters of the Euphrates (see Jer. 46:6-10; 47:2; 25:9-11, 15-26). In
Isa. 8:7, 8; 7:20 the flooding of the Euphrates referred to the
Assyrians coming to destroy Israel in Jerusalem. At that time the
attacking hosts of the Assyrians were destroyed by the miraculous
intervention of Israel's Almighty God (see Isa. 37:33-38, etc.). In the
last days, we are assured by the prophecy of Rev. 16:12 and Dan.
11:45, God will again intervene to save His people and destroy
their enemies. This message of comfort sent by our Lord through
His prophets, Satan seeks to hide, knowing that, with such strong
promises of victory over their enemies, the church will valiantly
face the foe, full of assurance in ultimate triumph.

The doom of Babylon, which was brought about by the
strategy of Cyrus drying up the river Euphrates, looms large in the
book of Revelation. This is the culmination of the Revelator's
depiction of the conflict of the forces of good and evil, just as the
ending of the king of the north is the culminating feature of the
prophecies of Daniel—both refer to the same thing. As the Revelator has already made reference in Rev. 14:8 to the overthrow of
Babylon by Cyrus's strategy, so his reference in Rev. 16:12 to the
coming of "the kings from the east" and the drying up of the
waters of the Euphrates must be understood in the light of his
previous reference (14:8) to the fall of Babylon.

The king of the north meets with great success (Dan. 11:40-45)
until Michael stands up, then the Lord intervenes and there is a
time of trouble such as never was. Similarly in the Revelation,
Babylon becomes exalted among the nations (Rev. 18:7, etc.). But
Christ intervenes, the seven last plagues are poured out: they are
God's judgments upon Babylon—including the sixth! They are "*her*
[Babylon's] plagues" (Rev. 18:4, 8). Therefore the symbolic drying

up of the Euphrates can refer *only to a judgment upon Babylon,* and cannot refer to the extinction of Turkey or nations adjacent to the literal Euphrates. As Babylon is world-wide, so the Euphrates upon which it was anciently built must also have a world-wide application. The plagues, described in Rev. 16, fall upon Babylon when Christ completes His mediatorial work in the heavenly temple. In Rev. 17 we are shown the *reason* for the Lord's judgments upon Babylon: they come *because of her persecution of the people of God.*

By comparing Rev. 12:12-16 with Rev. 13:5-7 and 12:17 with 17:1, 14, 15 we know that the Revelator describes the coming conflict of the combined forces of Babylon—kings and people—as the flooding of the Euphrates over its banks, threatening to engulf the people of God in ruin. There will be a mighty tide of persecution to turn them from their allegiance to the Lord. Rev. 16:12 refers to the Lord's intervention on behalf of His persecuted people. In their evil work of making "war" on "the remnant" church, the "kings" (mentioned in Rev. 17:13 as giving "their power and strength unto the beast") make *"war with the Lamb,* and the Lamb shall overcome them" (v. 14). That is, *because* they make "war" on His people, "the Lamb" will make "war" against the forces of Babylon (Rev. 19:11-21): this is referred to in Rev. 16:12-16 as *"the battle of* that great day of God Almighty. . . Armageddon."

Describing the coming destruction of the Jewish nation and of Jerusalem by the Romans, the prophet Daniel said: "the people of the prince that shall come shall destroy the city and the sanctuary; and the end thereof shall be *with a flood"* (Dan. 9:26). It is to this "flood" that the prophet again refers in Dan. 11:22. The Jewish nation with their beloved city, without the covering wing of God, went down under that Roman "flood." However, in the closing scenes of the great controversy, God's spiritual Jerusalem, "the true church," will be protected from the invading "flood" of the king of the north and his "multitudes. "

Pointing to the final conflict, the prophet Daniel directs our attention to the resurrected power of the king of the north who, recovering from the deadly wound inflicted on him by the king of the south in the French Revolution, goes "forth with great fury to destroy, and utterly to make away many" (Dan. 11:44).

Daniel likens the campaigns of the king of the north to that of the overflowing of a mighty river—the Euphrates (Dan. 11:40, *American Translation*): "The king of the north. . . shall sweep through many lands *like an overwhelming flood."* That "flood" will again surge "into the glorious land" (v. 41)—where God's people dwell—and, as in the time of the Assyrians, "the waters of the river [the Euphrates] strong and many. . . shall pass through Judah. . . even to the neck" (Isa. 8:7, 8). As a man nearly drowned by the inundating flood, with his head only above the swirling waters, so the city of Jerusalem, in the days of Hezekiah, seemed at the mercy of the invaders. But God intervened. The flooding waters were dried up. Thus shall it be when the king of the north floods into the antitypical land of Israel and reaches to "the glorious holy mountain."

The waters of the Babylonian "flood"—the waters of the great river Euphrates—will flood the land and threaten to engulf "the holy city" (Dan. 11:45; Rev. 11:2). But the Lord Who gave Daniel this prophecy "by the side of the great river"; that Lord Who stood *"upon the waters* of the river" when He made the solemn oath that He would end the persecution of His people (Dan. 12:5-7), will dry up the waters of "the great river" Euphrates" (Rev. 16:12): the king of the north "shall come to his end, and none shall help him" (Dan. 11:45).

CHAPTER TWENTY-NINE

CHRIST'S OATH: THE KING OF THE NORTH—
GOG FROM THE NORTH PARTS—
WILL PERISH FOR PERSECUTING HIS PEOPLE

B y a solemn oath (Dan. 12:7; Rev. 10:5-7), our Lord assures
His people that the king of the north will come to his end:
that his political and spiritual power to persecute will come
to an end, and that he will meet his doom in the last days. This
oath, given in the prophecy pointing to the doom of the king of the
north (Dan. 12:7), and mentioned in Rev. 10:5-7 in connection with
the rise and completion of God's last-day Message calling spiritual
Israel out of spiritual Babylon to the land of Israel, connects up
with the oath God made to Abraham that his seed would inherit
the land—see Gen. 15:7-18; Jer. 34:18; Gen. 12:1-7; Acts 7:1-5; etc. "If
ye be Christ's, then are ye Abraham's seed, and heirs according to
the promise" (Gal 3:29). Since 1844 spiritual Israelites have been
heeding the call of Christ to "come out" of spiritual Babylon (Rev.
18:4), and they have been spiritually gathering to the land of Israel.

In its spiritual application, the land of Israel means the place
where God's blessings are fully bestowed. "The Lord shall greatly
bless thee *in the land* which the Lord thy God giveth thee for an
inheritance to possess it" (Deut. 15:4). To spiritual Israel is given the
promise: "Now will I. . . have mercy upon the whole *house of Israel*. . . .
When I have brought them again from the people, and gathered them
out of their enemies' lands. . . Then shall they know. . . I have gathered them *unto their own land*, and have left none of them any more
there" (Ezek. 39:25-29). When "*the whole house* of Israel" shall have
"come out" of spiritual Babylon to the spiritual land of Israel, Satan
will stir up the hatred of all people of all nations to unite, or "gather
together," against God's people—see Ezek. 38; 39; Joel 3; Zech. 12; 14;
Rev. 16:12-16; 17:12-14; 19:11-21; Isa. 54:15; etc. This mighty assault
upon the people of God is pictured in the prophecy of Ezek. 38 and
39. In Rev. 20:8, 9 we are given the Lord's interpretation of this
prophecy: it portrays a vast gathering of those who are led by Satan
in his warfare against the city and people of God.

The King of the North at Jerusalem

To interpret this grand prophecy in relation to a military battle between nations to be fought in Palestine as "Armageddon" is to present a counterfeit of the Lord's presentation of the great conflict between Christ and Satan. This assault is made upon Israel because the Lord is *"in the midst of My people Israel"* (Ezek. 39:7). Before and after the millennium this graphic portrayal applies to the spiritual conflict—details of application the writer has enlarged upon in other publications. This mighty army attacking Israel under the leadership of Gog—Satan working through the Papacy and her confederates—is said to "come *up* [the mountains of Israel] from the *north parts*," or from *"the sides of the north"* (Ezek. 39:2, margin). The king of the *north* comes to slay the people of God— with him are all the people of "the whole world" (Rev. 16:12-16), but they are being thus led to their doom, for it will be "the battle of that great day of God Almighty."

After literal Israel came out of Babylon, and the "work of restoration had begun, and a remnant of Israel had already returned to Judea, Satan was determined to frustrate the carrying out of the divine purpose, and to this end he was seeking to move upon the heathen nations to *destroy* them *utterly*" (PK 583). "As he influenced the heathen nations to *destroy* Israel, *so in the near future* he will stir up the wicked powers of earth to *destroy* the people of God" (PK 587, 588). After the people of God had been called out of Babylon to "the land of Israel," Satan sought to persuade their enemies "to *destroy* them *utterly*." "As he influenced" then, "so in the near future" he will do the same. Then, Satan sought "to *destroy them utterly*." "In the near future" Satan will seek to destroy God's people "*utterly*." This, of course, is precisely what is mentioned in Daniel's last prophecy regarding the king of the north: "he shall go forth with great fury to *destroy*, and *utterly* to make away many" (Dan. 11:44).

"In the latter years" (Ezek. 38:8), Gog and his armies come "from the *north* parts" (Ezek. 39:2) to destroy the people of God. In the last days, the king of the *north* comes to destroy the people of God. That Gog and his armies refer to the same as the armies of the king of the north is obvious from the fact that both come from the north; both come in the last days; both come to destroy the people of God; both are destroyed by the God of Israel. Now the Lord has definitely told us that Gog's armies are the wicked who are led by Satan to war against "the holy city" and the people of God (Rev. 11:2; 14:20; 20:8, 9; etc.), so the same power who is referred to in Dan. 11 as the king of the north and who comes to attack the people and city of God, must also be the wicked who are led by Satan. In *The Certainty of the Third Angel's Message*, the writer has demonstrated fully the Bible principle of interpretation: before the millennium, the gathering of the forces of evil against "the holy city" is a spiritual representation (as if the church, being "the Israel of God," were in "the land of Israel"); after the millennium, the gathering of the forces of evil against "the holy city" refers to a literal gathering against the literal "Holy City."

The king of the north is Antichrist, "that man of sin, . . .the son of perdition; who opposeth and exalteth himself above all that is called God, or that is worshipped; so that he as God sitteth in the temple of God, showing himself that he is God." He makes a profession of representing Christ, but actually is against Him. He works "with all power and signs and lying wonders, and with all deceivableness of unrighteousness in them that perish" (2 Thess. 2:3-10).

In this power are worked out the principles of the proud Lucifer who, while professing to be prompted by noble motives, sought to exalt himself to *the place of Deity*: "*in the sides of the north*" (Isa. 14:12-14, compare with Ps. 48:1, 2). Gog and his armies come "from the *north* parts," from "*the sides of the north*" (Ezek. 39:2, margin). Gog assumes to be in the *place of the Deity*. Daniel declares that the king of the north "shall do according to his will; and shall exalt himself, and magnify himself above every god." This is the verse Paul quotes in 2 Thess. 2:3-7 when describing the Papal apostasy. In Daniel's last prophecy three powers are said to "*do according to his will*" The first (Dan. 11:3) was Alexander the Great who, after he had conquered Asia, encouraged the worship of himself as a god. The second (Dan. 11:16) refers to Rome under the Caesars who enforced Emperor worship. The third (Dan. 11:36) refers to the Papacy which exalts the Pope as a god and inculcates reverence for Mary. In this connection, observe carefully the following extract from the pen of God's servant commenting on ". . . the 'man of sin' foretold in prophecy as opposing and exalting himself above God. That gigantic system of false religion is a masterpiece of Satan's power—a monument of his efforts to seat himself upon the throne to rule the earth *according to his will*. . . . Satan worked *according to his will*" (GC 50, 51).

The name "Gog" means "covered," alluding to the deceitful character of him who bears this name. "Gog" is a fitting name for that false system of worship, which, under the guise of Christian nomenclature, continues, in the professedly Christian church, the old Babylonian mysteries associated with sun worship. It is a deceitful form of worship, for it counterfeits the true: it "covers" "the truth in unrighteousness," and changes the "truth of God into a lie" (Rom. 1:18, 25). Spiritual Babylon of the Revelation is the rival of Jerusalem, the spiritual home of God's people. The Lord calls His people to come out of Babylon to Jerusalem, the city of truth and peace (Rev. 18:4; Zech. 8:3). Though the head of that false system professes to be "the vicar of the Son of God," the Scriptures define him as "that man of sin. . . so that he as God sitteth in the temple of God [the professing Christian church], showing himself that he is God." Verses 6 and 8 of 2 Thess. 2 show that "Gog," the "*covered*" one, would be "*revealed*"; "then shall that wicked one be *revealed*."

How true are the footnotes in *Brown's Bible* concerning the prophecy of Ezek. 38; 39: "'Gog and Magog,' both signifying 'covered, concealed,' which, read in the light of 2 Thess. 2:3, 6, 8, where 'that man of sin,' 'that wicked,' is *yet to be revealed*—to be uncovered, as it were—and deprived forever of the mask of hypocrisy, that assumption of Christianity behind which is concealed his idolatry—his heathenism."

"Magog" meaning "expansion, increase of family," refers to the world-wide extension of Satan's false system of worship, which has "cast down the truth to the ground; and it [has] practised, and prospered" (Dan. 8:12, 24, 25). Error will so prosper that "*all* that dwell upon the earth [except the remnant church, Rev. 12:17, etc.] shall worship" the beast (Rev. 13:8). In the prophecy of Ezek. 38; 39, Gog's great army coming "from the *north parts*" represents the vast numbers of the unsaved. See Ezek. 39:12-16 and compare with Rev. 20:8, 9. In Daniel's last prophecy, referring again to the forces of evil making war against the people and city of God, attention is drawn to the great success attending the activities of the king of the north (Dan. 11:40-43).

The king of the north has not yet come to his end. The Lord warns His people by the prophecy of Dan. 11:40-45 and also by Rev. 13 to 19, that the Papacy will have a resurrection to power—all the political and spiritual power it has employed in the past, it will again employ in the final conflict. "The great controversy between good and evil will increase in intensity to the very close of time. . . . All the depths of Satanic skill and subtlety acquired, all the cruelty developed, during the struggle of the ages, will be brought to bear against God's people in the final conflict. . . . The coming struggle will be marked with a terrible intensity such " as the world has never witnessed" (GC ix-xi).

For a brief "hour" (Rev. 17:12), the king of the *north*, Gog "from the *north parts*," that man of sin, the son of perdition, the little horn, the beast, will wage a bitter "war" against the people of God (Rev. 12:17; Dan. 11:40-45). He will seem certain of his goal— the entire destruction of God's "holy city," Jerusalem: "He shall plant the tabernacles of his palace between the seas in the glorious holy mountain [*he will surround the church as the Romans surrounded literal Jerusalem to destroy it*]; yet he shall come to his end, and none shall help him"—no one will be able to help him, for He Who brings him to his end is no other than our Lord Jesus, "the great Prince which standeth for the children" of God, the Almighty Head and Deliverer of His blood-bought people.

CHAPTER THIRTY

THE TIME PERIODS OF DANIEL 12
FURTHER IDENTIFY THE PAPACY AS
THE KING OF THE NORTH

T hose who hold the view that the king of the north refers to Turkey are puzzled to know why the time periods relating to the Papacy mentioned in Dan. 12 follow the description of the ending of the king of the north. Uriah Smith asks concerning the 1260 days of Papal supremacy mentioned in Dan. 12:6: "Why is this period here introduced? Probably. . . To whom does the pronoun *he* refer?" *Daniel and Revelation*, p. 316.

Well might these questions be asked, for surely there would be no connection between the doom of Turkey (in supposed fulfillment of Dan. 11:45) and the 1260 years of Papal supremacy! Obviously, these time periods of Dan. 12 have a definite bearing upon the ending of the king of the north brought into the prophecy just before these time periods are mentioned. The pronoun "he" in Dan. 12:7 undoubtedly refers back to the king of the north who is designated in the previous verses by the pronouns "he" (mentioned 15 times), "his" (nine times), "himself" (twice) and "him" (twice).

Dan. 11:31-35 refer to the persecution of the church during the Dark Ages. Dan. 11:40-45 refer to the gathering of the forces of the Papacy for its final assault on the people of God. Hence the connection between the previous verses and the introduction of the time 1260 years of Papal supremacy in Dan. 12:7. Later in Dan. 12 other time periods are given relating to the Advent Movement which would prepare people to stand true to God in the final conflict, when the king of the north "shall go forth with great fury to destroy, and *utterly to make away many*" (*Dan.* 11:44). Concerning the original word for the expression "utterly to make away," Dr. Strong says: "The whole (spec. a *sacrifice* entirely ·consumed). . . whole burnt offering (sacrifice)." Newton says: "The original word we translate 'utterly to make away,' signifies to anathematize, to consecrate, to devote to utter perdition, so that it strongly implies that this war should be made upon a *religious* account." Thus the prophecy points forward to the time when the restored and revived Papacy will "go forth with great fury to destroy, and utterly make away many" of God's children, but the promise is that "at that time thy people shall be delivered."

One of the angels standing on the bank of the great river asks Michael the great High Priest, Who stands upon the rushing waters dressed in His priestly robes ("clothed in linen," Dan. 12:6; Lev. 16:4, etc.): "How long shall it be to the end of these wonders?" (Dan. 12:5-7). This question is repeated by Daniel (v. 8). "*How long*" will God permit the Papacy—the king of the north—to invade "the glorious land" and to attack "the holy city"? "*How long*" before the Papacy comes to his end? The time periods of Dan. 12:7, 11, 12 answer this repeated question.

Read in the light of Rev. 11:2 we know that Dan. 12:7 contains the prophecy that the king of the north would tread "under foot" "the holy city" for "forty and two months." At the end of that period he would come to the end of his political power—the king of the south would then "*push*" at "him" (Dan. 11:40), and render him powerless for a period. We know from such prophecies as those contained in Rev. 13 and 17 that the Papacy would receive a "deadly wound" which would render it helpless for a period, but that afterwards the "deadly wound" would be healed and all the world wonder "after the beast." Then, the attack upon "the holy city" would be renewed, and even with greater vigour than before (Dan. 11:40-45)—this time "utterly to make away" the despised people of God.

That this is the true interpretation of the climax of Daniel's last prophecy will be seen by noticing carefully the following application made by God's servant *of the deliverance* of God's people mentioned in Dan. 12:1:

"The wicked rushed upon the saints to slay them [Dan. 11:44]; but angels. . . fought for them. Satan wished to have the privilege of destroying the saints. . . but Jesus bade His angels watch over them. God would be honoured by making a covenant with those who had kept His law, in the sight of the *heathen* [this is an inspired comment on Ezek. 38:16, 23; 39:7, 23, 28; Joel 3, etc.] *round about* them [see Joel 3:12]; and Jesus would be honoured by translating, without their seeing death, the faithful, waiting ones who had so long expected Him. . . . God would not suffer His name to be reproached among the *heathen*. . . . He (would) manifest His mighty power, and gloriously *deliver* His saints. For His name's glory He would deliver every one of those who had patiently waited for Him, and *whose names were written in the book* [this is a definite reference to Dan. 12:1]. . . . The people of God, who had faithfully warned the world of His coming, would be delivered." EW pp. 282-285, chapter '"The Time of Trouble."

The question *"How long* shall it be to the end of these wonders?"* (Dan. 12:6) shows that Daniel's last prophecy concerning the king of the north came to Daniel in response to his prayers for more light on the previous vision (ch. 8 and 9). In Dan. 8:13, 14 is recorded a conversation between Gabriel and our Lord, just as in Dan. 12:5-7. In Dan. 8:13, 14 the question is asked by Gabriel, *"How long. . .* to give both the sanctuary and the host to be trodden under foot? And He said unto me, Unto two thousand and three hundred days; then shall the sanctuary be cleansed." The question in Dan. 8 relates to the work of the Roman desolator; the question asked in Dan. 12:6 relates to the king of the north who, also, is the Roman desolator. The question in Dan. 8 is answered by our Lord, saying: "Unto 2,300 days," then will the Roman desolator's desolations concerning the sanctuary and the host come to an end. The question in Dan. 12 is answered by our Lord, saying: "It shall be for a time, times, and an half; and when *he* [the king of the north is the antecedent] shall have accomplished to scatter the power of the holy people, all these things shall be finished," or, as given in the *Revised Version,* "When they have made an end of *breaking* in pieces the power of the holy people all these things shall be finished" (Dan. 12:7). Notice that this time period would bring us to the time when the king of the north would come to his *"end" of breaking in pieces the power of the holy people."*

In Dan. 11:14 the Romans are introduced into the prophecy as "the robbers," or *"breakers"* (see Dr. Strong, Bishop Newton, etc.) "of thy people." Literal Rome, the desolator, becoming the king of the north by conquering Syria, entered "into the glorious land," surrounded and destroyed Jerusalem, and broke in pieces and scattered the literal Jewish nation. Spiritual Rome, becoming the king of the north, in the Dark Ages, entered "into the glorious land," surrounded and attacked God's spiritual "holy city" (Rev. 11:2), and broke the power of spiritual Israel. Thus by the term *"the breakers,"* the prophecy in Dan. 11 regarding the king of the north is definitely linked with that portion of the same prophecy which is given regarding the Papacy in Dan. 12:7.

When the Revelator depicts the persecutions of the Dark Ages, he quotes from Daniel's last two prophecies and pictures the slain saints as asking *"How long,* O Lord, holy and true, dost Thou not judge and avenge our blood on them that dwell on the earth?" (Rev. 6:10). These martyrs were to "rest yet for a little season" (v. 11)—then the king of the north would come to his end. The question they are represented as asking refers, of course, to the last two prophecies of Daniel where the *same question* is asked *regarding the 2300 days and the 1260 days.*

Why are three time periods—1260, 1290, 1335—mentioned in the closing verses of the book of Daniel (Dan. 12:7, 11, 12)? Undoubtedly to bring before us the *commencement and endings* of the periods in relation to the power of the king of the north—the breaker of God's people. The terminals of these three periods *each point to an ending of the power of the king of the north.* The prophecy of Dan. 7 informs us that after the 1260 days of supremacy (Dan. 7:25) "the Judgment shall sit, and they shall take away his dominion, to consume and to destroy it *unto the end"* (v. 26). As we have shown elsewhere, the Lord based His second advent sermon upon these very prophecies of Daniel which we are at present considering. In Matt. 24:21 is the record of a statement which is in harmony with Dan. 7:26. He says: "For then shall be great tribulation, such as was not since the beginning of the world to this time, no, *nor ever shall be."* When the 1260 days ended the power of the king of the north to destroy God's people (as he had done in the Dark Ages) came to *an "end";* was *"finished."* This we have on the oath our Lord made in Dan. 12:7 in response to the question as to *"how long"* the king of the north would be permitted to break in pieces the power of the holy people.

The 1260 days commenced in A.D. 538. The decree of Justinian, issued in A.D. 533, recognized the Pope as "head of all the holy churches." The overwhelming defeat of the Ostrogoths in the siege of Rome, five years later, was a death-blow to the independence of the Arian power then ruling Italy, and was therefore a notable date in the development of Papal supremacy. With the period 533-538, then, commences the 1260 years of Dan. 7:25; 12:7, which would extend to the period of 1793-1798. The year 1793 was the year of the Reign of Terror in the French Revolution, and the year when the Roman Catholic religion was set aside in France. As a direct result of the revolt against Papal authority in the French Revolution, the French army, under Berthier, entered Rome, and the Pope was taken prisoner Feb. 10, 1798, dying at Valence, France, the following year. This period, 1793-98, during which this death-stroke was inflicted upon the Papacy, fittingly and clearly marks the close, of the long prophetic period mentioned in Dan. 7:25; 12:7.

The King of the North at Jerusalem

The 1290 days are mentioned in Dan. 12:11 because they connect up the time when, as brought to view in Dan. 11:30, 31, Papal Rome emerged out of the ruins of national Rome and became the spiritual king of the north. By its false system of mediation—the perversion of the priesthood of Christ—the Papacy has trampled under foot the truths concerning the sanctuary in heaven and the spiritual temple, the church, on earth. "The mystery of iniquity"—the counterfeit of "the mystery of Godliness" (1 Tim. 3:16)—was "already" working in the days of the apostle Paul. Basing his prophecy upon Daniel's last prophecy relating to the king of the north, Paul declared that "the man of sin" would sit "in the temple of God [that is, the church, see Eph. 2:21, 22, etc.], showing himself that he is God" (2 Thess. 2:3-5). The work of deception continued to blind the eyes of men to Christ's priestly ministry in the heavenly sanctuary. Finally, in 503 A.D., the Satanic errors were expressed by an official decree of an ecclesiastical council held in Rome, by which it was declared "that the Pope was judge as God's vicar, and could himself be judged by no one."

"The work of Clovis, king of the Franks" who earned for himself the title of 'eldest son of the church' by his campaigns to subdue the kingdoms hostile to the Papacy, contributed much toward putting into practical effect this claim of the Papacy, which finally resulted in establishing the Pope as the head of the Roman priesthood which has usurped the priestly work of Christ, and has established another system of mediation in its place. This work of Clovis came to its climax in the period 503-508, and this period therefore became the natural one from which to date the 1290 years of Dan. 12:11, which would accordingly end in the period 1793-1798, at the same time as the 1260 years of Dan. 7:25." *Bible Readings*, p. 229.

Employing the marginal rendering of Dan. 12:11, the text reads: "From the time that the daily sacrifice shall be taken away to set up the abomination," etc. That is, from the year A.D. 508 when by the victory of Clovis room and opportunity were provided for the establishment of the Papacy, until "the time of the end," would be 1290 days (literal years). After presenting evidence from numerous church historians, the author of *Daniel and Revelation* states: '"Thus in A.D. 508 terminated united resistance to the development of the Papacy" (p. 330).

Thus we are given the connection between Dan. 12:11 and Dan. 11:31, for both refer to the time when men would "take away the daily [ministry of Christ in the heavenly temple, and the knowledge of the true church, the spiritual temple, on earth], and they shall place

119

the abomination that maketh desolate"—the idolatrous Papal priest-hood. As literal Rome had destroyed Jerusalem and polluted "the sanctuary of strength," so the spiritual Romans attacked God's "holy city" and polluted the spiritual "sanctuary of strength." From Dan. 11:31 the prophecy is not to be interpreted literally in relation to the literal land of Israel. As the scene shifts from the literal Jewish nation, temple, and city to the heavenly temple and the spiritual temple on earth; from the literal Romans to the spiritual Romans, *so the rest of the prophecy must be interpreted accordingly*—as it relates to the people of God, and their enemies.

Seventh-day Adventists have no difficulty in following this principle in reference to the interpretation of Dan. 8 and 9. The prophecy of the 2,300 days commences with God's people heeding the call to come out of Babylon to repair the walls of Jerusalem and to restore the temple and its services; it ends with God's last-day Message calling His people out of spiritual Babylon to repair the walls of Jerusalem and to restore the truths concerning the temple and its services. The same principle must be applied when study-ing Daniel's last prophecy *which is the enlargement and explanation of the prophecy of the 2,300 days*. The connection between the 2,300 days and Daniel's last prophecy becomes more obvious when noting that the last time period—the 1335 days—given in the book of Daniel (12:12) brings us to 1844 as do the 2,300 days. The 2,300 days commenced with the decree (B.C. 457) permitting God's people to leave Babylon to return to their native land "to restore and to build Jerusalem" (Dan. 9:25); they end (1844) with the call out of spiritual Babylon "to restore and to build Jerusalem"—the spiritual "temple" and "holy city." In 1844 the 2,300 days ended: the Investi-gative Judgment commenced in heaven, and upon the earth God's spiritual temple began to be cleansed of the pollutions of sin and Babylonian errors. The 1335 days commenced A.D. 503-508 when spiritual Babylon, having passed a decree making the Pope the head of their idolatrous priesthood, thus officially commencing an attack upon the spiritual '"holy city" and "temple," was politically strengthened by the work of Clovis in subduing kingdoms hostile to the Papacy; they end in 1844 with the call out of spiritual Babylon to '"restore and to build Jerusalem"—the spiritual "temple" and "holy city." Beginning at the same date as the 1290 days (given in Dan. 12:11 to connect up with and to explain Dan. 11:31) A.D. 508, 1335 days (literal years) extend to 1843-4, the time when the world-wide proclamation was given, "The hour of His Judgment is come" (Rev. 14:6, 7). Light then burst concerning the ministry of our great High Priest in the heavenly sanctuary above.

From then the Papacy's deceptions concerning their false priest-hood were more fully revealed. The 1260 and 1290 days, which both ended in 1798, brought to an *end* the *political supremacy* of the king of the north; no longer would he have power to slay the saints as he had during that long period of persecution. The 2,300 and 1,335 days, or years, which both *end* in 1844, brought to an *end* the *spiritual power* of the king of the north to deceive people concerning the true priesthood in the heavenly temple and concerning the spiritual temple on earth.

Further Scriptural support for the position here presented regarding the *progressive "end"* of the king of the north may be seen by comparing the following texts:

Dan. 12:7: "He held up His right hand and His left hand unto heaven, and sware by Him that liveth for ever that it shall be for a time, times, and an half; and when he shall have accomplished to scatter the power of the holy people, an these things shall be *finished*."

Rev. 10:5-7: "Lifted up His hand to heaven, and sware by Him that liveth for ever and ever. . . that there should be time no longer. . . mystery should be *finished*."

In Dan. 12:7 the word *"finished"* has reference to the ending of the 1260 days in 1798 when *ended the political power* of the Papacy to persecute the saints. In Rev. 10:5-7 the application made of Dan. 12:7 is that, in 1844, prophetic "time should be no longer," for that would be the *end* of the longest time prophecy in the Bible—the 2,300 days of Dan. 8:14. But the complete application of Dan. 12:7 is seen in the statement, "'The *mystery* of God should be *finished*." That is, the end of *probation* when Christ has "finished" His heav-enly ministry. Thus by combining Dan. 12:7 and Rev. 10:5-7 we see that they refer to the *endings* of the three prophetic periods brought to view in Daniel's last prophecy—the 1260 and 1290 days ending in 1798, and the 1335 days ending in 1844. These periods were given to Daniel in order to clarify matters relating to the *ending* of the king of the north, which will occur after "the *mystery* of God should be *finished*" and "Michael" will have stood up and com-menced His kingly reign (Dan. 11:45; 12:1).

Spiritual Rome's power to "scatter" or *break* "in pieces the power of the holy people" was *"finished"* in 1798; her power to deceive true Israelites who accept God's last-day Message was *"finished"* in 1844; after "the mystery of God" is *"finished,"* then she would be *"finished"* with entirely.

That the last chapter of Daniel deals with the *ending* of "the days"—the 1260 *"days,"* the 1290 *"days,"* the 2300 *"days,"* the 1335 *"days,"*—pointing to the *ending* of the king of the north, is further indicated by the fact that the book of Daniel closes with the promise that Daniel (and those like him in character) would stand in his *"lot"* at the *"end of the days"* (Dan. 12:13).

The Hebrew word for "lot" is found 76 times in the Old Testament. Dr. Strong says of this word: " A portion or destiny (as if determined by lot)." See examples in Lev. 16:8, 9, 10; Num. 26:55; 33:54; 34:13; etc. Two main uses of this word are brought to view in the Old Testament: (1) Israel dividing the land by lot *before they entered into the promised land* (see Num. 26:55; 33:54; 34:13; etc.); (2) deciding which of the two goats employed *in the service of the Day of Atonement* should represent Christ or Satan. See *The Messiah in His Sanctuary*, p. 142, by F. C. Gilbert; *Daniel and Revelation*, p. 317; TM 115; PK 547. These authors show that the term is associated with the last message at the time of the Judgment—the *antitypical* Day of Atonement—*prior to Israel entering into the everlasting Canaan.*

"When Israel was about to enter into the promised land, the lot was cast, and the possession of each tribe was assigned. The tribes thus stood in their respective 'lots' long before they entered the actual possession of the land. *The time of the cleansing of the sanctuary corresponds to this period of Israel's history.* We now stand upon the borders of the heavenly Canaan, and decisions are being made, assigning to some a place in the eternal kingdom, and barring others forever therefrom. In the decision of his case, Daniel's portion in the celestial inheritance will be made sure to him. And with him all the faithful will also stand." *Daniel and Revelation*, p. 317.

Thus in Dan. 12:13—the last verse in the book—we are again reminded of the principle to be employed in the study of the book of Daniel—*the law of types and antitypes*. Though Daniel's last prophecy was not written with the same pictorial symbolism as revealed in the other prophecies, yet it can be understood only when read as if the church has taken the place of national Israel. In Dan. 12:13 the church is represented as if she were Israel on the Day of Atonement (when the scapegoat is to be banished from the camp, and Israel will be freed forever from all her sins) about to enter into the promised land. The expression *"thy people"* in Dan. 12:1 refers not to literal but to *spiritual Israel*. *"The glorious holy mountain"* of Dan. 11:45 refers not to the *literal* city of Jerusalem, but to "the holy city," "*the true church*" (GC 266). "The king of the *north*" does not designate a nation to the north of *literal* Jerusalem but to that *antitypical* power that emanates, *spiritually*, from the region of Babylon and the Euphrates "in the *north* country"; that power that assumes to *sit in the place of Deity* "in the sides of the *north*."

The prophecy of Dan. 10 to 12 was not given to describe events to occur in Palestine in the last days, but to describe the experiences of *spiritual* Israel in all the world—*in the antitypical, or spiritual land of Israel*—just before they enter into their eternal Canaan. "At the *end of the days*" mentioned in Dan. 12, the king of the north will come to his complete and *final end*. "At the end of the days" the people of God will enjoy their celestial inheritance: "at the *end of the days*" their immortal life begins in the springtime of eternity.

For further consideration of the books of Daniel and Revelation in relation to Seventh-day Adventists as the people of God, see the writer's book: *The Certainty of the Third Angel's Message Proved by Important Principles of Prophetic Interpretation.*

The following titles by Louis F. Were are also available:

The Certainty of the Third Angel's Message
The Kings That Come From the Sunrising
The Moral Purpose of Prophecy
*The Truth Concerning Mrs. E. G. White, Uriah Smith,
    and the King of the North*

More titles soon to come, including:
144,000 Sealed: When? Why?
Bible Principles of Interpretation
Christ Conquers, or Why Christ Rose on Sunday

To order any of these titles by Louis F. Were, or for a free catalog of books, videos, audio tapes and more at discount prices, contact:

Laymen Ministries

LMN Publishing International, Inc.
414 Zapada Rd.
St. Maries, ID 83861-9403

Phone: (208) 245-5388
Fax: (208) 245-3280
Toll free order line: 1-800-245-1844
email: lmnpubint@nidlink.com
Visit our website at www.lmn.org

Laymen Ministries/**LMN Publishing International, Inc.** is a self-supporting, privately funded 501 (c)(3) nonprofit corporation. We exist to encourage lay people in all parts of the world that, through being empowered by the Holy Spirit, they are the working force of the church, and are called to proclaim the Three Angels' Messages in our generation. It is our aim to help provide the necessary tools to accomplish this goal—to educate in practical religion, provide health education, assist in publication and distribution of literature, video, audio, and other media productions, etc. More information on our current international projects is available by contacting our office. Tax deductible receipts for donations are issued monthly.

More titles on today's hot topics in prophecy–

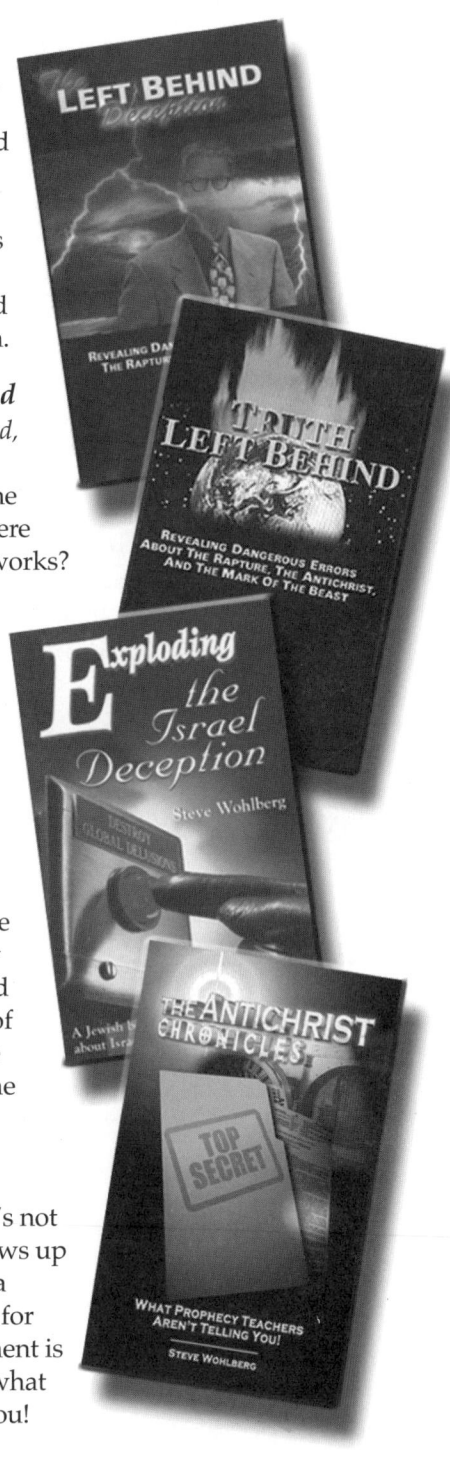

Pastor Steve Wohlberg has conducted Bible prophecy seminars in Russia, Canada, New Zealand, Pakistan, Africa, and all across America. He has taught thousands the importance of knowing Jesus Christ the Messiah and understanding the book of Revelation.

Left Behind and *Truth Left Behind*

Everybody has heard about *Left Behind*, the books and movie which present, through fiction, an interpretation of the prophecies of the last days. But are there serious Bible truths missing in these works? Worse, could a cloud of deception be settling upon the Christian world? (*The Left Behind Deception* is 3 chapters excerpted from *Truth Left Behind*, and is designed as a gift book to help the reader understand the origin of the rapture interpretation of prophecy.)

Exploding the Israel Deception

Millions of Bible students today have their eyes fixed on Jerusalem as they wait for the prophecies of Daniel and Revelation to unfold and the Battle of Armageddon to take place. Does the book of Revelation really focus on the Middle East?

The Antichrist Chronicles

This is not about fiction, but reality. It's not about an imaginary Mr. Evil who shows up after we're gone. Instead, is revealed a present Antichrist that's been around for centuries and which at this very moment is involved in global politics. Discover what the prophecy teachers aren't telling you!

An Adventist Apocalypse

By Ellen G. White

A compilation of hundreds of quotations from unpublished letters and manuscripts covering a wide range of issues and events that will confront the people of God in the last days. Much of this material is previously unreleased, nowhere else to be found.

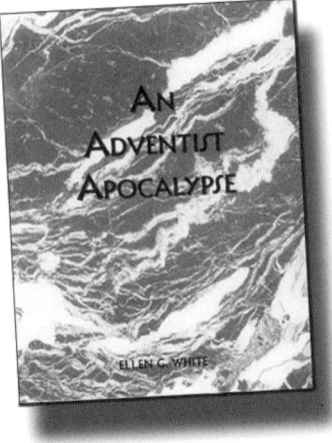

This is a paperback edition with easy to read type. Learn what God's messenger had to say about preparing for the coming conflict, the working of the enemy, the Latter Rain, events preceding the Second Coming, the Loud Cry, what will happen within the church, how God will sustain His children, the Judgment... and too many more topics to list. 160 pages.

Retail Price: $9.95 **Discount Price: $8.25** + S&H

The Sanctuary Series

Five *Sanctuary* volumes under one cover

By Arla Van Etten

Each detail of Type (earthly sanctuary) and Antitype (heavenly sanctuary) is presented side by side in an easily understood format, with texts and references for study. Designed for youth, but with ample content to provide adults with a fascinating, in-depth study, as well. Great for study groups!

240 pages, paperback. This edition contains:

The Young People's Sanctuary Series

    Volume 1:   The Camp Around
    Volume 2:   The Courtyard
    Volume 3:   The Offerings
    Volume 4:   The Tent Tabernacle
    Volume 5:   The Holy Days and Feast Days

Retail Price: $17.95 **Discount Price: $16.50** + S&H

Bible Students' Library

The Bible Students' Library series was originally published between 1889 and 1905, and was written by the Adventist pioneers. These booklets clearly present the principles of our faith. Excellent for your own study or for a witnessing tool. Most are under 30 pages and priced under $1.00, and all are small enough to fit in a pocket or purse. Additional savings when bought in lots of 100 or more.

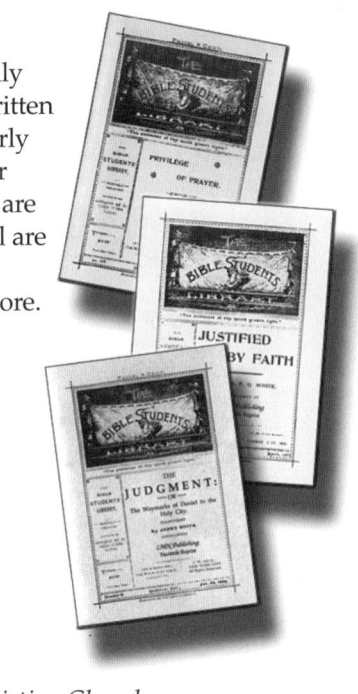

Includes such titles as:

Baptism, Its Significance
Can We Keep the Sabbath?
Christ Tempted As We Are
The Immortality of the Soul
Justified by Faith
Living by Faith
Privilege of Prayer
The Sufferings of Christ
Sunday: The Origin of Its Observance in the Christian Church
....and more....

Apples of Gold Library

Also written by the Adventist pioneers and published between 1893 and 1905 as tracts especially designed to fit in an envelope for mailing to friends and family. These little gems are excellent for your own sudy and for distribution in literature racks, evangelism, and personal witnessing.

Only $.25 each, or $.10 each for 100 or more.

Includes such titles as:

The Christian's Privilege
God's Word the Parent's Guide
Hope in Trials
The Power of Forgiveness
The Power of the Word
Three Sabbaths
What Must I Do to Be Saved?
....and more....

Who is

Laymen Ministries?

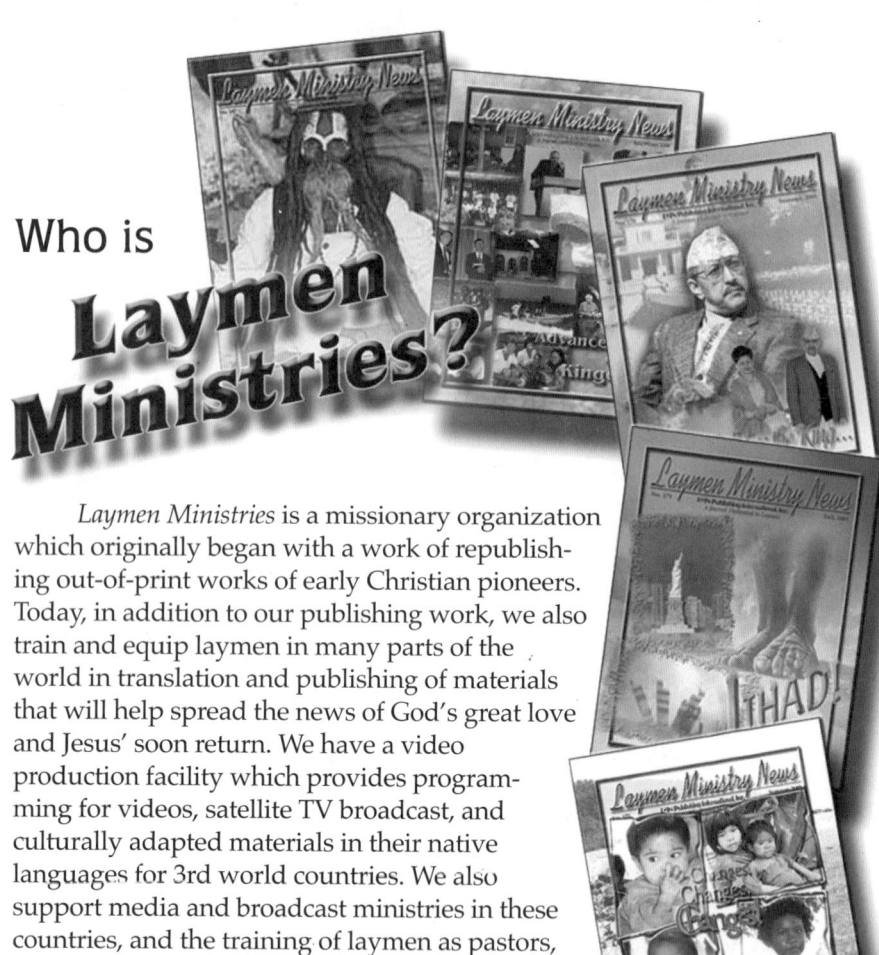

Laymen Ministries is a missionary organization which originally began with a work of republishing out-of-print works of early Christian pioneers. Today, in addition to our publishing work, we also train and equip laymen in many parts of the world in translation and publishing of materials that will help spread the news of God's great love and Jesus' soon return. We have a video production facility which provides programming for videos, satellite TV broadcast, and culturally adapted materials in their native languages for 3rd world countries. We also support media and broadcast ministries in these countries, and the training of laymen as pastors, Bible workers, and literature evangelists, as well as providing medical outreach and life-style training to help people live happier, healthier lives.

If you would like to learn more about the work we do, and about some of the fascinating projects we are involved in, please contact our office to receive your FREE subscription to our magazine, which contains exciting mission updates, as well as timely articles to strengthen and encourage laymen in all walks of life. We also offer a catalog with hundreds of books, videos, audios, and more at discount prices!

(208) 245-5388
Toll free order line: (800) 245-1844
Fax: (208) 245-3280
email: lmnpubint@nidlink.com
Visit our website at www.lmn.org